There's Always Room for *Cheese*

Colin Wood

Hardie Grant
BOOKS

Foreword

Colin is a curious, obsessive chef; his brain is simply wired differently.

During the years we worked side-by-side in New York City, he somehow always managed to carve out the time, no matter how busy we were, to seek out more knowledge and develop his own ideas and projects. And with this book, the effort has paid off. It's essential reading for anyone who is interested in deliciousness and the fundamentals that make it possible.

It's a reminder of what you can achieve when you work from scratch, slowly and well: a book about doing things the right way. The ricotta dumplings and nettles recipe (page 164) is an amazing example that is quite familiar to me, you could say. This dish draws on Colin's experience preparing versions of the recipe at Altro Paradiso and estela countless times, each attempt approached with presence and care. You start with fresh milk; four days later, there is a bowl of dumplings in front of you. It looks pretty unassuming. Then you taste it and discover how every step had an impact.

There's something like this to be found on every page. The way Colin encourages the use of pickles, ferments, and whey to impart flavor — or pairs a ribeye with a pungent cheese to bold effect — certainly leaves an impression. The same can be said for his craftsmanship, skill for cheesemaking, and commitment to farmers who follow an approach that positively impacts the environment, as well as your meal.

This book is the culmination of all of Colin's explorations and influences so far. But like all great chefs, he has built on these ideas and made them his own.

Ignacio Mattos, chef/owner and author, estela

Contents

Introduction

The art of cheesemaking has been around for thousands of years, and the topic is infinite. The history of cheese is rich with beautiful stories of provenance, tradition, technique, skill, flavour and more.

For me, I suppose you could call cheesemaking a hobby or, more accurately, a fledgling addiction. My cheesemaking journey started as a way of trying to deal with the stress, intensity and demands of working in professional kitchens. Learning and teaching myself something new allowed me to slow down, be creative, and to think about food differently.

This book comes from my experiences of making cheese, both at home and in professional environments. Woven among the information and recipes are stories and anecdotes about how I make, age, eat, share, care for and love cheese.

I hope you enjoy the book and, more importantly, the cheese you make.

Colin

Before we start

I am a chef first and a cheesemaker second. I began making cheese as a hobby some ten years ago and, in the time since, I have been lucky to have worked with some extremely talented, passionate and dedicated people in the fields of hospitality, food, wine and cheese.

I grew up in Western Australia and had an early career as an elite gymnast with aspirations of competing at the Olympics. However, at the end of my teenage years I found myself working in a hot and loud kitchen with aggression, discipline and hierarchy. With my background in elite sport, this was all so familiar that it was easy to slot right in and continue the search for excellence.

My nanna, Helen, and my mum, Maria, are of Polish/Ukrainian heritage, arriving in Australia after World War II. Nanna was a farmer and grew a lot of her own vegetables. She often would cook for us with the produce from her garden when I was little. Her dishes are family lore, and I can still remember the smells, sounds and flavours that permeated from her kitchen in Bassendean on the outskirts of Perth. I was a terribly fussy eater when I was young and it wasn't until I started cooking professionally that I began to understand and appreciate the lengths that Nanna would go to in preparing and cooking her soups, braises, schnitzels, peppers and cabbage dishes.

Starting at Andrew McConnell's Cumulus Inc. in Melbourne in 2007 opened my eyes to the provenance, integrity, flavour and good farming practices involved in each ingredient. Seeing the farmers turning up to the restaurant each week with their produce flicked a switch in me. Suddenly being a chef became more about the desire to cook with and eat good produce. The memories of Nanna's garden came back when I saw the tomatoes, broad beans, lovage and other amazing things coming through the doors, usually carried by the people who grew them.

I met Richard Thomas when I moved to the pastry station. If I thought Andrew and the farmers were passionate about what they did, Richard far exceeded them all. Often credited with being the godfather of Australian artisan cheese, Richard assisted many cheesemakers in the early 1980s to make specialty artisan and farmhouse cheeses. At the time I met him, he was running a small cheese-maturation room, importing younger cheeses from Europe and ripening them in his cellar for chefs.

With Richard as my newfound friend and mentor, I started to experiment and make cheese at home in my little one-bedroom apartment in Collingwood. I found the process so cathartic, so rewarding and so fascinating. It took hold of me.

Eventually I was able to incorporate my cheesemaking into my work and menus, and people started to follow, taste and get excited by my creations. This upskilling took me all the way to New York City to work with chef Ignacio Mattos.

While working in New York, I continued to make cheese at home. I met some lifelong friends and supporters, and I went to cheese parties, tastings, events, classes and anything that involved cheese. It was an exciting time for a curd nerd.

Cheese has now become such an integral part of who I am and what I do. It has taught me many lessons over the years and will continue to do so. I'll often find myself lying in bed at night wondering if I have flipped the cheese, or what to wash it in, or what I can create with it, or how much milk I should organise for the next batch. I'll often set my alarm for a late-night cheese flip or to straighten the cheese press, as the curds knit together overnight.

In the ten years since I first coagulated a pot of milk, I have made many wonderful discoveries and some awful mistakes too. The craft of cheesemaking is more of a skill than a talent. It takes work, time, commitment, good ingredients, specific tools and practice to make a decent cheese. The difference between my very first homemade haloumi and the grilled cheese that I make now is literally 'chalk and cheese'.

CHEESE TAKES TIME

To become cheese, milk goes through many transformations and, quite often, the process of maturation. Practice and patience will be needed, but it will be worth it.

One of the biggest misconceptions that people have when it comes to making cheese and dairy items at home is that it is very difficult. In some cases this is correct but like many things, you just need to start with the basics and go from there. To run, you must learn to walk first.

Making fresh cheese follows the same principles as making cheese that is aged for months and years. Obviously they are different, but they all start with quality milk, the right ingredients, consistent temperatures, time and safe food handling. Learning about the core ingredients, the science and the techniques is crucial to building the foundations to be able to make more varieties.

Not all styles of cheese are covered in this book, for example, blue cheese, hard cheese or the stretched curd–style mozzarella. Although these can successfully be made in the home environment, I have chosen to focus on the cheeses that I am most familiar with, have had the best success with, and am comfortable sharing with you. The recipes I've included take inspiration from the many places I've worked and the people I've worked with. My style of food and cooking relies particularly heavily on my time in Andrew McConnell's kitchens and, more recently, with Ignacio Mattos. I think you will be able to make them just as well, if not better, than me, if you carefully follow the instructions.

THE RIGHT TOOLS

As a trainee chef, you are told to choose the right tools for the job. As cheese has been around for thousands of years — long before the invention of plastic cheese moulds, stainless steel pots, ladles and thermometers — tools can be quite unique in the home environment. Specialty tools are available but, in my experience over the years, sometimes using your brain instead of a credit card is much more rewarding. Get creative and use what you have.

WHAT'S IN THIS BOOK

In this book you'll learn what cheese is, what it's made with, how it's made, how to make fresh and aged dairy and cheese, how to cook with cheese, how to serve it and how to care for it. There are also handy troubleshooting tips. I suggest you thoroughly read the background information in Chapters 1 to 4 first, then move on to the cheesemaking chapters. Decide which cheese you want to make and research what you'll need — start with a good milk supplier!

Maybe first try your hand at making the yoghurts and fresh cheeses and dairy (page 47) before moving on to the other cheeses in Chapter 6. You can then jump into the recipes in Chapter 8 (page 123) and make dishes using your own cheese creations. You can also make the recipes using store-bought cheese — just be sure to source your cheese from a good cheesemonger.

When a recipe calls for a certain type of cheese, it is usually because of the particular characteristic — flavour, pungency, saltiness, texture — that it brings. You could experiment and try making the recipe using a different cheese if you wish. In fact, one thing I would encourage you to do as much as possible is to play. Try different combinations, different styles, different textures, whether homemade or store bought.

One of the greatest pieces of advice and encouragement that I ever received is to try something and then try again. If cheesemaking has taught me one thing, it's that perfection is not achievable and a constant pursuit of it is pointless. You will stuff things up from here, trust me. I still do all the time. Just be kind to yourself and try again. Keep at it!

Cheesemaking *basics*

'A dairy product made by fermentation to safely preserve the nutrients in milk to be eaten and enjoyed at a later time.' That's what my jeopardy answer would be to the question 'What is cheese?'

Cheese is made up of just four ingredients — milk, rennet (or another coagulating agent), good bacteria and salt. Cheesemakers can add or omit ingredients to achieve certain things. Some cheeses don't have rennet, some don't have added bacteria, some are fresh, some are aged, and some add herbs, spices, seeds and other things to achieve flavour and texture.

The essential ingredient, milk, contains two major proteins — casein and whey protein, and when the milk starts to acidulate and the pH of the milk drops, the two start to separate, forming 'curds and whey'. When carried out in a controlled way, this process protects the milk from spoilage by making a less hospitable environment for certain organisms and allowing the good bacteria to thrive. When milk starts to sour naturally because of its age or temperature, bacteria in the milk grow quickly and break down the lactose, producing lactic acid. The casein forms lumps (curds), and separates from the liquid (whey) giving the milk that horrible smell as it goes off. Cheese is actually made the same way, except the process is sped up to lower the pH in a more controlled, safer and delicious way.

The milk is brought to a certain temperature and the bacteria present, or added, start to convert the sugars in the milk — lactose — into lactic acid. Rennet is added to coagulate and set the milk, then once the curds and whey are separated, the milk — as American author Clifton Fadiman said — is on its 'leap toward immortality'.

To safely preserve cheese and dairy products for periods of time, microbes work in a variety of roles, from converting the lactose, producing gases and moulds, growing rinds on the surface to protect the cheese, the ripening of it, to giving the cheese its unique flavour, texture and aroma. Salt is also a key element in making cheese delicious and safe, as it provides flavour, encourages good bacterial growth and is used in numerous ways to help in preservation.

Cheese has been around for thousands of years in many different forms across the world and is one of the oldest food sources known to humans. It is a beautiful combination of history, science and craft, with thousands of variations and stories from farmhouse and artisan producers to large, industrial-scale production. In the beginning, cheese was made by hand on the land and gave rise to the many varieties and styles seen today, some of which are still made in those same early ways. Cheese that is made on the farm, where the animals are grazing and milked with little to no automation, are called farmhouse or farmstead cheeses. These terms come from New World cheesemaking and are used to define a genre of cheese that is very much old world in practice. The environment, animals, feed and milk is the top priority with the cheesemakers being in full control and understanding what is happening on the farm. In my opinion, these can be some of the purest, most raw, flavourful and honest cheeses being made, with taste and profile at the forefront of their production. Often passed down from generation to generation, inherited or taught, cheese made on the farm – especially with raw milk – aims to give a true taste of place and, in a lot of cases, cultural perspective and significance.

But not all farmers can make and age cheese on their properties, and not all cheesemakers can milk and maintain a farm, and so artisan cheese is the next step from farmhouse production. Historically, and more specifically in French history, cheese was a symbiotic relationship between a farmer, a cheesemaker, an affineur (see page 22) and a cheesemonger. The farmer would provide the milk, the cheesemaker would turn the milk into cheese, the affineur would age the cheese and the monger would sell the cheese. This process still happens in many places. Artisan cheese, like most artisanal products, is primarily made by hand in small batches – the milk is bought direct from a small farm, the use of machinery is limited, and the level of care and skill involved is high. The focus, as with farmhouse cheese, remains on the quality of the ingredients and the flavour of the cheese. And then there is industrial or commercial cheese.

While the two previous categories of cheesemakers recognise and understand that pasture raising, regenerative agriculture and animal welfare are central to the quality of their cheese, large-scale commercially produced cheese is more about manufacturing large volumes of cheese for consistency, marketability and longevity.

While artisan producers are looking to make cheese that reflects the environment and the milk, commercial cheese is on a much larger scale, often using co-ops of milk, which often leads to homogenisation and standardisation of the cheese and dairy produced.

Now, just because a cheese is farmhouse or artisan it doesn't mean it's delicious – some can be an acquired taste. As an early 80s kid, I've seen and eaten more than my fair share of yellow, plastic-wrapped, mass-produced cheese. However, through my own discovery of cheese and what good cheese is, I've experienced how well-made cheese can influence the palate, a dish or meal, an industry, a community and the environment. Good cheese is good for everyone. Cheese in the New World is exactly that, new. Australia, Canada, New Zealand and many other colonised countries all share a similar story of their cheese DNA. Cheese is predominantly Old World, and most cheeses take their origins and roots from the rich histories and tapestries of Europe and Asia – even the cheddars that started it all in these 'new-found' lands.

For Australia, although there were cows on the first of the British ships that colonised the land of the First Nations People, early cheesemaking was very limited until the late 1800s. Cheddar was the predominant cheese being made in England at the time, and with the arrival to Australia of Henry Harding – the son of Somerset cheesemaker Joseph Harding, also known as the 'father of cheddar cheese' – an industrial cheese factory was established in Bodalla, New South Wales. Henry believed that cheese needed to be consistent, made to have a long shelf life and be easy to distribute across the vast land. His cheese wasn't produced on the farm but in the factory, and thus Australia's love affair with large factory-produced yellow block cheese was born and remained that way until the 1980s when a small group of cheesemakers set out to make and sell their own styles of artisan cheese.

With travel, stories and inspiration from the great cheeses of Europe, and the assistance of Richard Thomas, artisans like Milawa, Tarago River and Meredith Dairy began producing cheese in the east, as did Gabrielle Kervella in the west with her farmhouse goat's cheese. These were the pioneers of the artisan cheese movement in Australia: those who paved the way and inspired the next generation of cheesemakers to pick up a curd cutter and make cheese. Some of these iconic producers are still making cheese, and the small-scale farmhouse and artisan cheese movement has grown steadily to now include farmhouse producers such as Holy Goat, Pecora Dairy, Bruny Island Cheese, The Pines Kiama, Drysdale Cheeses and Cambray Cheese.

The US went through a similar renaissance in the late 70s and early 80s, when a group of passionate women across the country began making goat's cheese. While both the US and the Australian cheese revolution was brought about from travels abroad, the goat's cheese movement in the US also stemmed from a more holistic approach to farming and using the milk that was being produced. Laura Chenel in Sonoma, California, Mary Keehn at Cypress Grove, also in California, and Judy Schad at Capriole in Indiana were some of the first to make cheese in this way. In a testament to what they achieved, some are still producing the wonderful goat's cheeses that showed American chefs and the public what good cheese is and could be. Their hard work and dedication in pushing through many barriers and obstacles enabled a boom in the field of artisan cheese, increasing public awareness and embellishing a taste for quality, well-made cheese. Old Chatham Sheepherding Company, Adante Dairy, Vermont Shepherd, Spring Brook Farm, Grafton Village Cheese Co, Parish Hill Creamery and Jasper Hill are just a tiny handful of the producers doing special things with milk and cheese across the US – all of which I've been lucky to work with.

The seven types of cheese

All cheese is not equal and can be broken down into categories, with many overlapping for various reasons. However, there are seven broad categories of cheese:

Fresh
Pasta filata
White mould
Washed-rind
Blue
Semi-hard
Hard

Some may argue that processed cheese is an eighth category, and perhaps they are right, but then I don't suspect many of you reading this far have that thought. Nuts aren't cheese — they don't lactate, and they certainly don't produce casein to make cheese. Neither do seeds or vegetables, so vegan cheeses aren't included in this book either.

FRESH CHEESES are exactly that — fresh with a high moisture content, and best eaten as soon as possible because they don't have a long shelf life. These styles are often very simple yet bursting with flavour, especially when a good milk source is used. They can be cultured to add complexity, flavour and longevity or made simply with fresh milk. Fromage blanc (fresh white cheese), fromage frais, ricotta, cream cheese, quark, mascarpone and labneh all fit in this category along with many more. They can be made with most milks and are a great starting point for creating your own cheese at home.

A ripe white mould cheese.

PASTA FILATA, meaning 'spun paste' in Italian, are cheeses that are made by forming a curd, then heating and stretching it to form soft, delicate and rich curds. They are usually quite high in fat and moisture and have a short shelf life in fresh form, so are also best eaten straight after being made. However, caciocavallo, provolone and a few other styles in this category can be hung and aged. There are many beautiful stretched-curd cheeses around the world, including mozzarella, fior di latte, burrata, oaxaca, bocconcini, braided styles such as majdouli, and even haloumi. Cheeses in this category are pulled and stretched at a higher temperature after the curd has been acidified, which gives the cheese that delicate, stringy, stretchy glossiness and higher melting point. Making them well takes time, patience and practice as well as a solid pair of calloused hands. Generally, milk with a high fat content is used, as in the case of buffalo milk for traditional mozzarella (fior di latte is actually what the cow's milk version of mozzarella is called).

WHITE MOULD CHEESE refers to the category of surface-ripened soft cheese covered in white mould with an undergrowth of surface bacteria. These cheeses are usually small and round with a high moisture content. Brie, camembert, Brillat-Savarin, Coulommiers, Crottin and the many locally produced fuzzy cheeses throughout the world fall into this category. Ripened from bacteria and the mould-covered exterior inwards, these aged cheeses are generally quite young and, depending on the size and shape, can mature within two and ten weeks of production. Once the mould has developed on the outside, the cheeses are wrapped to slow the growth and keep them moist while they are ripened to the core until they are soft and, in some cases, very oozy and decadent. White mould cheese can be made with any type of milk and can also be mixed to give different flavour profiles to the finished cheese.

WASHED-RIND OR SMEAR-RIPENED CHEESE can be soft or semi-hard and comes in all sorts of sizes and shapes. These are the pungent and damp cheeses that can be rich and oozy or firm enough to grate. Washed in brine solutions, beer, wine, cider, brandy and other alcohols, these cheeses usually have specific bacteria that give them their signature orange/brown moulds, aromas and exteriors. Bacteria called *Cornyebacterium or Brevibacterium linens* (*B. linens*) is often used or found on these styles and it is these bacteria that give these cheeses their familiar colouring and pungency, while also aiding in breaking down and softening the cheeses as they age.

Some of these soft, creamy and aromatic styles can also be called monastic cheese, as many years ago they were made by monks and nuns in Italian and French monasteries as a means of income and sustaining their communities that religiously abstained from fish and meat as a source of protein. As many were also producing wine and beer as a source of income the cheeses were often washed with alcohol, giving the cheese moisture, colour, flavour and an acquired taste. Taleggio, Reblochon, Époisses, Soumantrain, Pont L'Évêque and Munster are all examples of monastic cheeses.

A green cheese ready to start the ageing process.

Typically enjoyed in the cooler months, there are also some very unique cheeses made with autumn/winter milk in Europe and the US. They are wrapped in bark, washed and then aged until they are rich and soft in the centre. Mont d'Or, Rush Creek Reserve from Uplands Cheese, and Winnimere from Jasper Hill are some very good examples, along with a recent addition to Australian cheese, Driftwood, which is being made in Victoria by Long Paddock. These styles are not only good to serve as is, but are also great to cook with, bringing punchy, pungent, earthy flavours and richness to recipes and dishes.

BLUE CHEESE can be soft, firmer, young, older, sweet, savoury, fudgy, creamy, crumbly, mild or pungent. These cheeses are usually light and pale in colour with blue and green veins streaking through the cheese and sometimes on the rinds. These are produced with moulds called *Penicillium roqueforti* and *Penicillium glaucum*, which give the cheese its colouring, flavour, aromas and characteristics. It is a beautiful style of cheese that is often perceived to be an acquired taste or one to avoid in the new world, yet it is revered in France with Roquefort, in Italy with Gorgonzola, and in the UK with Stilton. A good blue cheese is difficult to make but is something that can change the perceptions of the non-admirers. Made with cow's, sheep's or goat's milk, blue cheeses have a rich history within cheesemaking, and are generally high in moisture content and acidity with the curds not usually cooked or pressed to allow for the *P. roqueforti* moulds to penetrate and proliferate the cheese. Cheesemakers usually keep these cheeses separate from others when they are made, as *P. roqueforti* moulds are very easily transferred to other cheeses and that can be an issue. Two very fine examples of well-made cheeses in this category are both made with raw milk — Bayley Hazen Blue from Jasper Hill in Vermont, US, and Stichelton, made by Joe Schneider in Nottinghamshire, England. These definitely changed my perception of blue cheese.

SEMI-HARD CHEESE is probably the largest category of cheeses. Cheeses of this style can be quite young, or aged for some time — even up to two or three years. They are made by cutting, cooking and pressing the curds and drawing out the whey and more moisture than the softer styles. This reduction in moisture allows the cheese to be safely aged for longer. Alpine styles such as Comté, Gruyère and Beaufort fall into this category, along with gouda, Raclette, Ossau-Iraty, Tomme-style cheese and many more. The use of raw milk in these styles is very prominent throughout the world, and because of that lower moisture content and longer ageing, they are considered 'safer' by many worldwide authorities and so are available in most countries. A quality farmhouse semi-hard made with raw milk is a thing of beauty and a delight for the palate and senses. Cheeses in this style can also be made with a variety of milks but are a little more difficult to make and age at home.

HARD CHEESE is self-explanatory. These cheeses are the large, robust, drier, firmer, flavoursome and often crumbly styles of cheese that, due to their size and age, take hundreds of litres of milk to make. The curds are cut smaller and cooked at a higher temperature, drawing out even more moisture, thus allowing the cheese to be aged for much longer and for more flavour to develop. They are challenging to make and age well but, when done right, as in the case of Parmigiano-Reggiano, they are a real testament to the art of cheese and the craft of the cheesemaker. As these cheeses age, little pockets called tyrosine crystals can form and provide wonderfully gritty, white pops of umami flavour that make you want to eat more. Because of the length of ageing, some of these styles are wrapped in bandages or cloth and lard or fat to protect the cheese while allowing it to breathe and develop flavour and mould growth, while others are dipped in wax to minimise mould growth on the surface. Others, such as gouda, are dipped in wax to minimise mould growth on the surface — a technique introduced for the purpose of exporting cheese on slow boats.

Dry salting and brushing semi-hard cheese.

WILDFLOWER
BREWING&BLENDING

The cheesemaking process

Milk goes through a few steps on its way to becoming cheese, with the type of cheese being made determining what steps and processes are used. Cheese can be made by acidifying the milk, either slowly by culturing, or quickly with direct acidification via vinegar or acid. It is then coagulated with rennet, heat and/or acid to form a curd and then, depending on what the cheesemaker is making, it is gently scooped or cut, stirred and separated from the liquid whey to firm up.

Some cheeses, such as Gruyére, Grana Padano and Parmigiano-Reggiano, are cooked, meaning the curds are warmed to release more whey and moisture, then drained and placed in baskets and hoops to form their shapes. They can be pressed, or can simply drain with gravity, depending on the final moisture content of the cheese being made. Aged cheeses are salted on the exterior to draw out more of that moisture and to promote good bacterial growth for the rinds to develop.

Fresher styles of cheese, such as fromage blanc, have a much higher moisture and lactose content because they do not go through the cutting, cooking and exterior salting processes and therefore are not suitable for ageing. Aged cheese is basically about controlled dehydration, and as the cheese ages,, the lactose content continues to reduce. Hard cheeses, such as Parmigiano-Reggiano, aged cheddar and gouda have very little lactose left, if any at all.

1. RIPENING Milk is warmed, cultures become active or are added, and acidification begins. When adding cultures blooming them first helps distribute them evenly and consistently. This refers to the powder slowly absorbing the milk or liquid.

2. COAGUALTION – SETTING An enzyme called rennet is added to the milk to form a solid mass known as curd.

Cutting the curd.

3. CUTTING This is when the solid curd mass is cut with a curd knife into cubes to begin releasing the whey. Before you make the first cut, you need to look for a 'clean break'. This is when a small cut is made in the set milk by sliding either your finger or a knife at a 45-degree angle, to separate the curd. If the whey runs into the crack, then you have a clean break. If not, leave for another 10 minutes and try again. When the solid curd is ready, make cuts by gliding the curd knife from the top to the bottom, from left to right, in increments and then back to front, so you end up with squares when looking at the curd from the top. Then cheese is cut on a 45-degree angle to form cubes of curd. Some recipes call for several cuts, decreasing in size each time to draw out more whey and moisture. Depending on the style of cheese and the moisture content required, the curds are kept larger and more delicate, or stirred and cooked to draw out more whey and moisture for a firmer curd that will age longer.

Smearing mould and beer onto cheese.

Affineur

Affinage is a French term that loosely translates to 'refining' and refers to the unique skills used to refine and age cheese. Someone who ages cheese is an affineur (a-fin-ER). If cheesemaking is the making of the blank canvas, affinage is the actual art. Maturing a cheese is a highly skilled craft, and an affineur's job is to manage and manipulate the changes in the cheese to achieve the desired outcomes. Cheese is alive and, as it evolves, its environment needs to be controlled and kept stable, much like that of humans. We like it when the environment and temperature is consistent, and so does cheese. Cheese needs to be flipped often to control its moisture and balance and it needs to be washed, rubbed and/or salted to manage and promote mould growth. The affineur's job is to look after and encourage the characteristics of each cheese. Salting, turning, washing and scrubbing can take hours and needs to be done regularly. The affineur works just as hard as the farmer and the cheesemaker to bring the cheese to market.

4. STIRRING/COOKING A white mould cheese retains moisture as the curds are gently cut into large cubes and stirred, with the finished curd being the size of a large grape and still soft — the delicate texture of a just-set jelly. The curds are kept at a consistent temperature throughout the process, enabling the microbes to be active and continue their work. The curd for a semi-hard cheese is cut smaller and handled more robustly; the temperatures of the curd and whey are steadily raised over a period of time to draw out more whey, cook and firm up the curd and increase the activation of the thermophilic bacteria. The finished curd may be much smaller, about the size of a lentil and firm to the touch. The size and texture of the finished curd is important for ensuring the cheese has the desired outcomes.

5. HOOPING/DRAINING Once the curd is at the desired texture and size, it is scooped, ladled or flipped into perforated baskets and hoops of all different shapes and sizes to further drain and then, in some cases, it is pressed. Hooping is the trade term for placing the curds into the baskets and hoops to form their shapes and sizes and to knit together. Small baskets are generally used for softer styles of cheese, whereas the larger, firmer aged cheeses go into metal or wooden hoops, often with lids (called 'followers') to press the curd down to form the cheese.

6. SALTING Salt is added for flavour, to help preserve the cheese and also to aid in forming a rind. Dry salt can be added to the fresh curd or applied to the rind of a cheese, or the cheese can be immersed in a brine solution.

7. AFFINAGE This is the ripening or maturation stage and in the right hands allows the cheese to reach its full potential. It requires a good temperature-controlled environment of 8–14°C (46–57°F), a good amount of humidity and low airflow.

Ash is often used to protect cheese, reduce moisture, increase pH and speed up mould growth, especially with goat's cheese.

The cheesemonger

The cheesemonger comes in at the final step in the cheese production chain. Their job is one of great importance and quite often is part of the affineur's role, since they create temperature-controlled environments in which the cheese may finish ripening or be stored until it's ready to be sold and eaten.

A good cheesemonger is passionate, knowledgeable and dedicated to serving as the link between everyone involved in the making of the cheese and the consumer. Their role is hugely important, especially in the world of artisan cheese, as they are the ones who source the cheese, share the stories, the history, the making procedures and the romance of the local, interstate and international cheeses stocked in their cabinets and fridges. They are usually well travelled, well informed and have in-depth knowledge of the origins of each cheese, the farm, the cheesemakers, what's happening with the seasons and the nuances of each cheese.

They can also help you on your cheesemaking journey with insights, feedback, encouragement and support. When I was starting out and had no idea, a friend and monger in Melbourne, Anthony Femia, was a constant cheerleader and sounding board. He still is. You should find a good cheesemonger to befriend.

When you buy your cheese from a respected cheesemonger, you are not only getting access to the best cheese in its prime, but you are able to become better educated and help build and foster the relationship between everyone in the life cycle of cheese.

At farmer's markets, you may find that the cheesemonger who is talking to you about the grassy, cave-aged, aromatic and delicious piece of cheese that you just bought, was also responsible for farming, making and ageing it.

As educated and mindful chefs and consumers move towards buying seafood from reputable fishmongers, meat from quality grass-fed farms and artisan butchers, local heirloom and organic varieties of fruit and vegetables from farmers and markets, it should be the same for cheese, milk and dairy.

289

Milk – the essential *ingredient*

When I was a kid, milk was my worst nightmare, so if it was strange for me to get into professional cooking, it was even stranger that I fell in love with cheese and dairy. For me it was and still is the history, stories and practices that got me interested in making and learning about cheese. Hearing about transhumance (moving livestock to different grazing grounds in summer and winter) for the first time when eating a piece of L'Etivaz (see page 27), researching the stories and histories of each remarkable cheese, and learning about the breeds of animals and the different cheeses that they produce, and the importance of provenance and terroir in cheese was all so intriguing. However, I do think it was listening to Melbourne cheesemaker Richard Thomas talk so passionately and knowledgeably about the core ingredient – milk – that intrigued me most of all.

There is always so much attention and focus on other ingredients and products in professional kitchens that I had never thought about where the milk comes from. 'Don't you just pick up a carton or plastic bottle at the supermarket?' I asked. 'No,' Richard insisted.

Milk is very much a 'live' ingredient. Just as lobster starts to deteriorate as soon it is taken from the water, milk declines in freshness and quality from the moment it leaves the animal's teat. It is at its peak just after milking and starts to slowly break down from there, until it eventually sours and curdles. Therefore, the best milk for cheese is undeniably raw milk, still warm from the animal, and if it must be stored it should not be too chilled – low temperatures are not good for the bacteria in raw milk.

Once an animal is milked, the milk is either used raw in cheesemaking, preferably within a few hours, or – as Australia and a few other countries for consumption – legally pasteurised, a process that uses heat to kill off pathogens.

Quality raw milk is the best ingredient for cheese-making. However, it can be quite difficult to legally procure. So, for the purposes of the recipes in this book, any milk referenced is pasteurised. But please don't let that stop you if you have access to raw milk.

When a cheesemaker says 'fresh' milk, they mean as close to milking time as possible. Therefore, making cheese can be difficult in cities, so it is a good idea to go to farmer's markets, befriend a processor or visit a local dairy farm to get your milk. Building relationships with dairy farmers may also provide you with opportunities to learn about the area, the farm, the farmers, the animals and what is happening with the seasons. On my cheese journey I have been fortunate to meet some truly special folks who farm and milk their own animals. Using their milk to make cheese has always been a pleasure and has produced good cheese. There are people out there on the land doing wonderful things, so find them and support them.

Milk is a funny thing in that you will not be able to tell how old it is when you get it, and it will pretty much smell the same all the way up until it spoils and you have a bottle of curdled milk. Then you will definitely be able to smell its age!

Milk is made up of fats, protein, lactose, minerals, vitamins and water. Like a lot of ingredients, milk is seasonal and therefore the composition and makeup of milk is constantly changing. Its quality differs from day to day, even from morning to evening. There are many factors that influence the properties of milk, including the type of animal, its breed, age and health, its feed, the number of daily milkings and the seasons and local weather conditions.

For farmhouse and artisan cheesemakers, it is all about the milk. The breed of animal, what they are eating, how they are being cared for, the environment they are living in and how the milk is processed is all extremely important. A lot of cheeses throughout the world are only made with certain breeds in certain regions – for example, Manchego is only made with Manchega ewe's milk, Comté from Montbéliarde or French Simmental cows in the Jura, and Camembert de Normandie from Normande cows in Normandy. The list of breed, locale and process-specific cheeses is extensive, and these are often protected by DOP, AOP or PDO status, much like Champagne and Prosciutto di Parma.

L'Etivaz, an alpine-style favourite.

Wine and cheese are not only good to enjoy together, they share a beautiful thing called terroir. Terroir is a French word that refers to the taste of a place and refers to the influence a region may have on the grape or, in this case, cheese. Climate, soil, grass, temperature, humidity, and bacteria on the animal and in the air are among numerous factors that can impart flavour in a cheese through the habitat and milk of the grazing animal. Many cheeses are named for the towns and regions they are made in because of this. What the herd is grazing on greatly influences the milk and gives the cheese its nuanced flavour profiles. For example, L'Etivaz is an alpage-style cheese, meaning it is made high in the Swiss mountains using raw milk from the herd grazing on summer alpine pastures. The flavour is incredible, as is the story, methods and history behind this cheese (see opposite).

Grass-fed, free-ranging animals that drink clean water and are milked once per day produce good milk. It goes without saying that any dairy animal that is cared for, treated well and raised on a good pasture outdoors is going to produce great milk. That's why it's best to find a farmer, or your own cow, goat, sheep or buffalo to milk. Then you will also find out how the different seasons affect the availability, volumes, variations and proteins in the milk, and how complex it all is. There are plenty of resources, tools and research out there if you wish to learn more, and I recommend you do. *Reinventing the Wheel* by Bronwen and Francis Percival is a good place to start.

The commercial milk-making processes

Other processes also affect the milk and resulting cheese. Pasteurisation, homogenisation and separation for skim milk all alter the properties of milk. So does cooling the milk down. Raw milk is used very close to the milking time or kept tepid, with 14°C (57°F) considered the ideal temperature for milk intended for cheesemaking. Over time, many processes have been introduced and industrialised to fill the supermarket shelves with a huge array of different milks and labels. So what do they all mean?

- PASTEURISATION is the heating of raw milk to certain temperatures to kill off bacteria and micro-organisms, followed by rapid cooling. This can be done at a high temperature for a short period of time, or at a lower temperature for longer.
- HOMOGENISATION is where the fat globules of milk are broken up by passing the milk through fine valves or nozzles at high pressure. This process disperses the fat through the milk and stops the cream separating and rising to the top.
- SEPARATION Traditionally milk would be left out so the cream and fat would rise to the top to be skimmed off, creating a lower-fat milk. These days centrifugal separation is used to achieve this, which enables processors to control fat percentages in the milk. This is why the supermarket aisle is loaded with so many options, brands and labels: skinny, low-fat 2%, half and half, and the list goes on.

L'Etivaz

Each year as the winter snow dissipates and spring blossoms, a small group of generational cheesemakers, along with their herds, start their transhumance journey and head up the Vaud alps to make a very special cheese. Starting in the 1930s, these defiant cheesemakers broke away from Swiss mandates and standardised Gruyére production to band together and build a co-op and ageing facility that to this day protects and promotes their own distinctive cheese.

Transhumance is a very old practice used throughout the world and involves moving the herd and animals to higher pastures in summertime, so the herders and farmers can use the lower-lying valleys to grow and produce their food. It is a cause for celebration, with parades and festivals occurring both on the way up in May and then again in September/October when the herd is led back down the mountain for the Désalpe de L'Etivaz. A cheering crowd gathers to give thanks for a good grazing season, with the cows adorned with flowers, bells, mirrors and for the 'Kranzkuh' or leading cow a cross.

L'Etivaz, made over open fire in copper cauldrons, with raw alpine pasture milk containing wildflowers, herbs and the lush green grasses from May to October, takes on the typical sweetness and caramel notes of alpine cheese with a slight smokiness from the fire. There are many alpine cheeses that are made in a similar way to L'Etivaz, but none are quite as traditionally driven, raw and beautiful.

To taste L'Etivaz is to experience traditional cheesemaking at its most pure - it can transport you to those alpine summer pastures. It is simply one of my favourite things to eat.

I do recommend that you try this cheese and research it for yourself, along with all the other cheese that you enjoy. The history, practices — and lengths that the cheesemakers go to preserve them — are remarkable. It will also give you a greater understanding of why good cheese is expensive.

The best places to source milk

Buying milk from a large supermarket is always going to be a challenge in cheesemaking. As the milk usually comes from numerous farms, and will most likely be a couple of days old when you get it, it could have all sorts of things going on. Most industrially produced cheese is made with milk from many different breeds on different feed from different locations and this can make the cheese quite generic and flavourless. Each breed and animal also has different fat and protein levels. For example, the fat and protein content of the milk from a Guernsey cow is much higher than that of a Jersey. Milk found in a supermarket is mostly standardised to provide for a more consistent product and doesn't allow for the variances and influence on flavour that come from using a single breed and herd on pasture. In my experience, a small farm working in a positive, regenerative way, really caring for their herd and land, can really provide a great quality milk.

That doesn't mean you won't be able to make cheese with store-bought factory milk, it just may not give you as quality a product and may not coagulate or set as well. The calcium content of milk can deteriorate when going through the pasteurisation and homogenisation processes, as well as with age. This results in a slower coagulation after adding the rennet, a softer less stable curd, and can even result in the milk not setting at all. This can be quite frustrating. Calcium chloride can be added to homogenised or calcium-deficient milk in cheesemaking to counterbalance this, but most often you won't know if you need to add it or not. At this point you are probably thinking how strange this all sounds – pasteurising a good raw product, then adding calcium back into it because it's calcium deficient. It gets even more strange when you add microbes back into the pasteurised milk to start the fermentation process and add flavour, but more on that later.

So where should you source milk, cream and dairy?

You can try visiting farmer's markets or small markets and/or building relationships with local farmers and doing some research into what is available. Good milk can be quite tricky to find at times, but there hasn't been a city or town I've lived in where I haven't been able to find a source. Look online for farm gates or hobby farms and websites that collate such information. There are some great resources out there, and more and more people starting to produce good milk, some of which even pops up in small supermarkets and grocers.

By sourcing direct from the farm or as close to as possible, you will not only be helping a small farmer and their family out, but you will be getting quality fresh milk that you can trace. Hell, if you show enough interest, you might even get to milk the animal yourself.

I was very lucky early in my cheesemaking journey to have met and worked with Ben Evans and St David Dairy in Fitzroy, Melbourne. Ben's commitment to restoring an age-old tradition of a local milkman sourcing quality milk was quite a revelation in inner-city Melbourne at the time. A fourth-generation dairyman, Ben supplied many cafes and restaurants with milk, cream and butter and had a small factory about a fifteen-minute walk from my apartment. In the early days I would wheel my little shopping cart to the front window, push the doorbell and pick up five bottles to take back home and make cheese with.

Ben and his wife, Bianca, sourced their milk from a pasture-based farm with organic practices about 100 kilometres (62 miles) from the plant in rural Victoria. The business was built on transparency, ethics and a commitment to quality over quantity, and I really admired that. In the early days of their business, Ben would pick up the milk early in the morning, hand-bottle it and deliver the milk himself, often sleeping in the factory for a few hours before starting again. It was this commitment to the milk, the farm, the business and the community that drew me in to learning more and building a friendship that has lasted ever since. Ben's unwavering support and genuine excitement for whatever I was making or playing with encouraged and inspired me to keep experimenting. Besides, if I stuffed something up, I'd be back down there the next day looking for more milk.

After an inspiring trip to San Francisco to spend some time in the ferment, pickle and cheese wonderland of Bar Tartine, I started making cheese, fermenting milk and playing with all sorts of dairy things at Cutler & Co. and Marion wine bar. Having Ben and St David just down the road not only made things very convenient, but enabled me to have quality fresh milk to make cheese with. And I made quite a lot.

So, if you really want to make good cheese, first find yourself a good milko.

Types of milk

Not all milk is created equal and not all milking animals are indigenous to their environments. As mentioned before, cows, sheep, goats and livestock have only been in Australia for a relatively short time. Different species and breeds are found throughout the world with some being introduced and others being endemic to their regions. There are thousands of cow, sheep, goat and buffalo breeds, but not all of them are suitable for milking and cheesemaking purposes. In some parts of the world, milk from yaks, camels, horses and donkeys is also used to make cheese and dairy other products.

Popular dairy cow breeds found in Australia, the US and UK that produce good milk are Jersey, Holstein-Friesian, Brown Swiss, Guernsey and Ayrshire. There are many others used specifically for cheese throughout the world.

Goat's milk may come from Toggenburg, British Alpine, Saanen, Lamancha, Nigerian Dwarf, Anglo Nubian or Sable breeds but, again, there are many other breeds that are milked, particularly in Latin America and the Mediterranean.

The East Friesian and Awassi breeds are the most common and productive dairy sheep in Australia and the US. Friesland, Lacaune, Assaf, Sarda and Chios are also used throughout the world, with Spain having many native breeds that produce some of the most well-known sheep cheeses – the Manchega breed giving us Manchego, and the Italian Pecora Sarda breed being responsible for Pecorino in Sardinia.

There are also many buffalo breeds, predominantly the river buffalo, suitable for dairying. These are found throughout the world, especially in India, Pakistan and South-East Asia, where their milk is the predominant dairy source.

The composition of milk

Milk is mostly water, with its properties differing with each species, breed and season.

COW'S MILK generally has a fat content between 3.5% and 5%, with Holsteins on the lower spectrum and Guernsey and Jersey breeds at the higher end. Jersey milk can sometimes exceed this and may reach as much as 5.5%. The protein percentage can range between 3.4% and 3.9%, with lactose making up around 5%. Cow's milk also contains beta-carotene, which is a pigment that gives plants and vegetables an orange colour. Picked up from the grass, the pigment gives grass-fed cow's milk – especially that of a Guernsey cow – that bright yellow colouring in their cream, butter and cheese. A single cow, with a lactation cycle of approximately 305 days, can produce up to 20–24 litres (5–6.25 gallons) per day, depending on the many factors a farmer has to navigate on a daily basis within the herd.

GOAT'S MILK is relatively similar in composition to cow's milk and has around 4% fat and 3.4% protein. Goat's milk is naturally 'homogenised', with smaller fat molecules suspended in the milk, as opposed to being separated as in cow's milk, so the cream does not rise to the top when left to settle. Goats can produce on average between 2 and 3 litres (quarts) of milk per day in the lactation cycle of approximately 280 days, and sometimes more when they are well fed and cared for.

SHEEP'S MILK is high in fat at 7.5%, with protein at 6%, making it good for cheese and yoghurt making. The higher fat content contributes to a richer, fuller mouthfeel and smooth texture, while a higher protein increases the yield of the firm curd when the cheese is being made. A single sheep can produce between 1 and 3 litres (quarts) per day, with many factors contributing to this, especially at the busy lambing time of year. The amount can sometimes be higher but with a shorter lactation cycle than that of a cow or goat, at approximately 100 days, making sheep the most difficult and least efficient to farm.

BUFFALO MILK also has a high level of fat at approximately 7%, but a lower level of protein at around 3.8%. Of all the milks used for cheese and dairy, buffalo milk comes in third highest in lactose percentage at 5.1% and, like goat's milk, is naturally homogenised. With a much higher content of milk solids than cow's, buffalo milk is used for mozzarella, stretched cheeses, yoghurt, ghee, paneer and more fresh varieties. The yield of buffalo milk is significantly lower than a cows, despite their size, at usually 6–7 litres (6¼–7¼ quarts) per day with a lactation cycle up to approximately 295 days.

Unlike cow's milk, the milk from goats, ewes and buffalo all convert the beta-carotene found in grass and feed into vitamin A before milking, so their milk and subsequent cheese is always white.

ANIMAL	FAT %	PROTEIN %	WATER %	LACTATION CYCLE
Cow – Jersey	5	3.9	85	~ 305 days
Goat	4	3.4	88	~ 280 days
Sheep	7.5	6	80	~ 100 days
Buffalo	7	3.8	83	~ 295 days

Table adapted from *The New Rules of Cheese* by Anne Saxelby

Cheesemakers use all sorts of milks with varying levels of fats, proteins and makeups to create their cheese. Some take the fat out, then add amounts back in to standardise the milk for production. This can be done for consistency, flavour, texture and, in some cases, because that is what is required in order for the cheese to be called by a certain name.

FOR THE PURPOSES OF CHEESE

The closest milk to raw is unhomogenised milk, so I like to use that for most of my cheesemaking. However, you could use any quality milk available to you.

Boiled water
Calf rennet
P.C.
Brevi
Flora

CHAPTER 3

Rennet, salt and other *ingredients*

Now that we have established that good milk is the most important ingredient in the cheesemaking process, we are left with rennet, salt and bacteria to transform the liquid milk into a solid mass, then into cheese.

Each of these ingredients plays an important role in the process of curd production, and can be used in conjunction with each other in the making of more mature and aged cheeses or even for simply separating the milk solids and whey with vinegar, as in the case of whole-milk ricotta.

Rennet

The story goes that thousands of years ago rennet was most likely discovered by herders storing and transporting milk on long journeys in vessels. The milk was being curdled in the vessels, which were made from either calf, lamb or kid stomachs and thus rennet was found.

Animal rennet is a naturally occurring set of enzymes that allows for casein molecules to knit together, forming a solid curd. It is obtained by extracting the enzymes from the fourth stomach chamber — known as the abomasum — from young, unweaned ruminants, typically a calf or kid goat. The abomasum is cleaned, salted and dried to make liquid, paste or powdered rennet.

This process has been around for millennia and is a very natural and organic way of obtaining rennet to give a good set curd, especially for traditional or natural cheesemakers such as David Asher, who also shows home cheesemakers how to do it in his book *The Art of Natural Cheesemaking*. I also prefer animal rennet, store-bought in liquid form, and the recipes in this book are made using calf rennet.

Now you can probably understand why vegetarians ask what kind of rennet is used to make the cheese they are about to eat.

Artichokes, nettles, cardoons and some other thistles also contain enzymes similar to those found in animal rennet and can be used to coagulate milk. Suitable for vegetarians, historically these weren't as well suited to setting a good strong curd and could sometimes leave a bitter aftertaste in the finished cheese, but over time they have been developed to be much more consistent. Fig and caper leaves have also been used to set milk — I am yet to work with either of these, but I'm sure there are recipes and methods that work well if you choose to use them. (The fig leaf cheese on page 173 uses animal rennet to set it — the fig leaf is just there to impart flavour.)

There are many very good examples of cheese made with vegetable rennet, and due to improvements and advancements in the setting capabilities, many cheeses — especially in the New World — are being made very successfully vegetarian.

Lastly, there is microbial rennet, which is made in a lab from mould, fungus or yeast and not from animals, making it good for vegetarians. It is usually cheaper and can have a longer shelf life than animal and vegetarian rennet.

MEASURING RENNET

With advancements continually being made in the cheesemaking world, all three types of rennet are viable options in liquid, powdered, paste or tablet form to make cheese. They are all different and require different dosages so check the labels when using them. Rennet can be single, double or even triple strength, meaning that smaller amounts of the stronger ones can have the same effect as larger amounts of a lower-strength one.

Milk measurements also differ throughout the world with the US using gallons and quarts in the imperial system, which can make the translation of amounts and measurements even more confusing. Most of my cheesemaking uses millilitres (ml) for measurements, but if you are from the US you may be more comfortable measuring small amounts in cubic centimetres (cc), or using drops from an eyedropper.

1 millilitre = 1 cubic centimetre = 20 drops
therefore 0.5 ml = 0.5 cc = 10 drops
and 0.25 ml = 0.25 cc = 5 drops

When you buy your rennet it will say how much rennet to use for an amount. You will need to use your calculator and maths skills to figure out the ratios and amounts needed for each cheese and volume. For example, some liquid rennets may call for 2 ml or 2 cc of rennet to set 10 litres (quarts) of milk, while others may call for 2.5 ml or 2.5 cc to set that same 10 litres.

Always check what the label recommends and follow the instructions. Do this before you start your cheese.

Add rennet, then stir well to disperse it through the milk.

Because rennet is so strong, it should be diluted in non-chlorinated water before adding to milk. This helps it disperse more evenly. Most rennet will also have instructions as to the dilution ratios. If you don't have filtered or spring water, you will need to boil and cool tap water before using it to remove any chlorine.

The seasons, species, age, temperature, acidity and properties of the milk, along with the rennet, amount and cheese you are making, can all alter the set time and curd consistency. Sheep's and goats milk, for example coagulate faster than cow's milk. It is not one size fits all, and cheesemakers adapt their recipes according to these factors. A flocculation test is used as a way of finding out the precise setting and cutting time of curd. However, for the purpose of the recipes in this book, it's been kept relatively the same.

Starter cultures, bacteria, yeast and mould spores

Remember the pasteurisation process that kills off certain bacteria in milk (page 27)? Well, that also kills off the good bacteria that are responsible for a cheese's flavour. A starter culture is a cocktail of good bacteria that begin the breakdown of lactose into lactic acid and give the cheese its flavour and character. While some raw-milk cheese producers do not add any cultures to their milk, pasteurised milk needs these to aid in the acidification, ripening and development of the cheese.

Direct vat inoculation (DVI) or direct vat set (DVS) cultures – usually in powdered or granular form – are manufactured in labs and can be very consistent for producing cheese. However, when pasteurised milk is used, and the cultures available are limited, this can contribute to the homogenisation of cheese and a reduction of characteristics.

Natural cheesemakers, on the other hand, grow, maintain and use their own cultures to produce their cheese. Comté is one such cheese and shows the complexity and flavour that, under the skillful watch of the cheesemaker, is achieved by using native and natural cultures with raw milk. In the US, Parish Hill Creamery and Jasper Hill, among a few others, are making their own cheeses with their own cultures. With a bit of luck, cheesemakers in Australia, and other countries where raw milk is a hot topic, may also be able to work with raw milk and cultures to produce cheeses in this way.

Think of these manufactured cultures a bit like yeast for a baker. They will give you a consistent, safer and more manageable cheese but with compromise. Kefir, yoghurt and clabber are also good sources for introducing microflora to cheese and if you want to get wild and funky with your cheesemaking, David Asher is your guy. His research, book, work and education in this field for home cheesemakers is inspiring and brilliant. Most of the recipes in this book are made with bought cultures, but they can also be made successfully with a more natural approach. DVI and DVS cultures pack a punch, so most recipes in this book require a minute amount – a little goes a long way.

Different cheeses require different temperatures for the good bugs to work best. Fresher, younger and softer styles of cheese, such as fromage blanc (fresh white cheese), brie, camembert and even Stilton and other blue cheeses, which aren't required to be cooked, need bacteria and yeasts that are most active at lower temperatures – between 20 and 32°C (68 and 90°F) – and these are called mesophilic cultures.

Cheeses made at higher temperatures require bacteria and yeasts that love warmth and are active when the milk and curds are heated and cooked. These are called thermophilic cultures and are more active at higher temperatures – up to 50°C (122°F). These are the ones to use for cheeses such as mozzarella, provolone and cooked-curd varieties.

These cultures are available online and in health-food stores, and can be quite expensive. They also have expiry dates and need to be kept clean and dry.

Cultures with bacteria and yeasts are alive and love consistent temperature – too warm they begin to die and too cold they go to sleep. It is important to maintain temperatures when storing them and especially when making cheese. Store them in sterile containers in the freezer, labelled and dry, for best shelf life.

Flora Danica and Type B starter are mesophilic, medium-temperature starter cultures that are used for flavour and acid production, particularly with sour cream, cultured butter and softer cheeses. Cultures containing gas-producing bacteria (*Leuconostoc*) are favoured for blue cheese.

Dry salting and brushing the rinds of firmer cheeses encourages development and control of mould growth.

Type C cheese starter is a high-acid producing thermophilic starter that is used with mozzarella, stretched curd and other cheeses, which speeds up lactic acid production with cooking of the curd.

Penicillium candidum and *Geotrichum candidum* are white mould spores that are used to introduce the moulds to the cheese either in the milk production stage or afterwards when the salt is added to encourage the mould growth. Blue mould spores are also used in the form of *Penicillium roqueforti* for the production of blue cheese.

Brevibacterium linens and *Corynebacterium* are naturally occurring bacteria used in the production of washed-rind cheese to aid in flavour, aroma and colour.

Salt

Salt is a mineral that is processed from two sources — seawater gives us sea salt, while salt mines are responsible for rock salt. Salt is not only essential for human and animal health but for curing and preserving food, such as cheese and charcuterie.

Salt plays a vital role in cheesemaking in many forms. It not only helps impart flavour into the cheese, but it also helps to draw out moisture, aids in controlling bacteria in the cheese, and helps preserve and protect it as it matures.

Salting a cheese can be done dry or wet, and this really depends on the cheese.

DRY SALTING is where the salt is rubbed onto the surface of the cheese and helps younger cheeses, such as white mould styles, to release more whey while allowing the mould and rind to develop.

WET BRINING helps the larger and more aged wheels to draw in the salt for flavour and to develop their rinds after drying out.

Salting and rubbing help the affineur control and manipulate mould growth on cheese and encourage the rinds and bacteria to develop and, in some cases, be more dominant.

Salt can also be used to aid in preventing spoilage and promoting longevity, as in the case of haloumi and feta in brine. It's also why some of the long-aged cheeses such as Parmigiano-Reggiano can be left out for lengthy periods and have longer expiration dates.

Salt for cheese needs to be non-iodised with no additives, such as anti-caking agents. Iodised salt is salt that has been sprayed with iodine, which inhibits mould and bacteria growth and slows the ageing process drastically. A good non-iodised flaked sea salt or cheese salt is best.

Time: the final ingredient

There is a fifth and final ingredient vital to a good cheese — one that I am beginning to appreciate more and more — and that is time. You will need to make time to make cheese, to look after it and to enjoy it. Cheese really forced me to slow down, to think about things in a considered way, to plan better, to enjoy the process and to enjoy the time with myself.

You can get more milk, more culture, more rennet and more salt whenever you need, but time isn't renewable or cheap. It really is the most important resource, so use it wisely.

The cheesemaker's *toolkit*

You can make cheese in a bucket with a thermometer and a ladle, or you can spend thousands of dollars on expensive equipment. I started with a small pot, a couple of cheese baskets and a dodgy pair of scales that had a thermometer probe wired to them. This is where the romance of cheesemaking lies for me — the transformation of milk from liquid to solid, in a small setting, working with what you have and a bit of MacGyver-like ingenuity. Commercial cheese factories are quite often large shiny, stainless-steel, sanitary operations where the picturesque associations and grandeur of cheesemaking can be missed.

After the years of experimenting at home and in restaurant settings, and seeing the production rooms of small cheesemaking businesses, I can say there is no right or wrong tool, instrument or way to make cheese. There's usually a better way, though, and if you constantly work on finding it, you might just get there one day. Sometimes I wonder if those cheesemakers high up in the mountains, using fire and copper cauldrons the same way for hundreds of years, find new things out each day. I'd like to think so.

I've used large pizza paddles, hardware buckets, immersion circulators, laundry sinks, open fire, induction cooktops, pasta colanders, kitchen spiders, cutlery drawer trays, a wooden wine box and even the shirt off my back once. The quote, 'If it means something to you, you will find a way' often springs to mind when I think back on some of the 'tools' I've used to successfully make cheese.

However, the items covered in this chapter are the basic tools required for making cheese.

The vat or vessel

Cheesemakers use vats or vessels to make cheese on a larger scale, but these are neither ideal nor cost and space effective in a home or restaurant set-up. Buckets or stainless-steel pots work just as well and can be heated in a similar fashion as an industrial water-jacketed vat, where hot water is circulated around the outer layer of the vat to warm the milk inside. When warming the milk, you can heat indirectly via a sink full of warm water just as the vat would, or directly by heating with a flame or induction.

Direct heating can cause the milk to scorch and burn, especially in large volumes. It can also heat the bottom too rapidly, leaving the milk at the top to heat slowly — so keep an eye on it and the milk moving. Heating in a water bath allows for a more even, slow heat distribution — this method is more consistent but can use a lot of water.

The idyllic connotations that people often associate with cheesemaking can be quickly quashed when entering a modern facility, with all the stainless steel and mechanisation used to produce at scale. However, there are still plenty of cheesemakers making cheese with traditional methods, using open fires, large copper cauldrons, large paddles, whisks and raw grit to make their cheese with a real love and care for the craft.

Thermometer

Invest in a good thermometer and make sure it's calibrated. I prefer a digital model, such as a Thermapen with a long probe, so the temperature can be measured more evenly. It needs to measure between 4 and 100°C (39 and 212°F) and be precise. Use it often to check the milk temperature and the exterior temperature too. Remember the cheese bugs like a constant and even temperature just like us. A thermometer with a timer attached to it is not a bad idea, as timing is also crucial in cheesemaking.

Previous page, clockwise from left: log basket, petite cheese basket, haloumi/feta baskets, bamboo brush, handmade cheese knife, bamboo mat, cheese trier, brush

Syringes

Depending on the amount of milk you are using, syringes are a good tool for measuring out liquid rennet. Rennet is a strong enzyme and not much is required: 0.2 ml (0.2 cc) can set 1 litre (34 fl oz/4 cups) of milk. Pharmacies and drug stores usually stock these from 0.5–10 ml (0.5–10 cc) and they are reusable until the numbers fade, in which case you can mark them, but it's best to replace them to be accurate.

Ladles and spoons

Maybe it's the chef in me, but I prefer stainless steel in one solid piece to stir and move the milk. Using plastic, wood, bamboo or utensils that have joins can provide more opportunities for dirt and bacteria to creep in, and while everything is constantly sterilised during cheesemaking, reducing the risk helps. A small set of measuring spoons is also handy but not necessary. There are mini spoons available online with very small measuring specifications right down to a 'smidgen'.

Curd cutter knife

A long blade, knife or palette knife is a good substitute for a professional curd cutter. Its length will depend on how deep your pot or vat is, as the curd needs to be cut from the top of the curd to the bottom and then laterally.

Sterilisation equipment

Touching your equipment or exposing it to other surfaces gives unwanted bacterial the opportunity get into your milk and cheese. A boiling pot of water is most effective for sterilisation. Keep the water boiling and change it as needed. Always give your utensils, baskets, hoops, cloths, and any other items that come in contact with the milk or cheese, a good wash in hot, soapy water before dipping it into the boiling water before and after use.

Cheese baskets or hoops

Commercial cheesemakers use plastic or stainless-steel hoops, baskets and followers (lids) due to the ease, uniformity, cleanliness, availability and strict regulations surrounding cheese manufacturing, while traditional, home and natural cheesemakers have been using wooden, thatch, woven, ceramic and plant-based baskets since cheese was first made. These are what provide the cheese with its shape and curd structure while the whey continues to drain.

Plastic is reliable, reusable and easily accessible but not the best for the environment. Baskets and hoops can be fashioned out of many things in a home kitchen space, and it is quite a fun afternoon drilling and concocting baskets out of household goods.

Old yoghurt tubs, small buckets, stationery trays and other small plastics can be repurposed and drilled to make draining baskets. Wooden boxes too. Small wicker baskets are also good for cheese, and some talented ceramists are making and selling cheese hoops for the home cheesemaker too. A tip: when drilling the holes for your baskets, drill from the inside out so the inside is smoother (you could also sand the rough edges back).

Smaller moulds and baskets are usually for softer styles of cheese, with small holes for draining, while the larger moulds, called hoops, are for the more aged styles that require more milk, pressing and time for maturation.

Draining table

Once the curd and cheese is hooped, it needs to continue draining. Bamboo mats, perforated trays and stainless-steel or plastic cooling racks with elevated legs sitting in a tray work well in the home or restaurant kitchen. In a commercial setting a large stainless-steel bench on an angle with a chute at the lower end is used to allow the whey to run off. Depending on the depth of your tray, you might need to drain the whey from time to time, as you don't want the cheese sitting in a pool of whey.

Cheesecloth

Kitchen cloth (such as Chux or J-cloth) is horrible stuff when it comes to cheesemaking. It is used everywhere in kitchens and has got to be one of the industry's biggest waste issues alongside plastic and plastic wrap. Where does it all go? Surely it must take a long time to break down and, aside from all that, curd clings to it and it's very difficult to clean. Cotton muslin or cheesecloth is much better. It's machine-washable, reusable and lasts for ages if looked after properly. Head to a draper and buy it by the metre (yard) or find it online.

Cheese press

Larger, more aged cheeses often require pressing to help the curds knit together and push out more whey after they've been hooped. You can buy a small home one online, make one or get crafty and use large tins, flagons filled with sand or water or even gym weights. They are not as steady as a proper cheese press, so keep an eye on the cheese as it's pressing, as it may tip over. If it does, don't stress too much – just readjust it and further press to realign.

Cheese cave

Cheese needs a constant, controlled temperature and humidity to ripen well. This can be achieved in a home or restaurant environment by using tubs, draining racks and a small temperature-controlled wine/charcuterie fridge or walk-in wine cellar. A converted fridge can also give the desired effects and there are many online tutorials and notes about doing this with thermostats and humidifiers. Speak to a fridge mechanic, as they often love doing stuff like that.

The tubs need to fit the cheese but also allow for air circulation and the cheese to be raised from the bottom. A small air hole is needed at the top to further allow for circulation and to trap humidity in the 'cave'. The fridge should be kept somewhere that has good airflow, and a moderate ambient temperature around 10–16°C (50–60°F).

The senses

Use these often. Look, taste, feel and smell as you're making cheese. You will start to recognise the lactic smells of acidification, the flocculation and coagulation, the sweetness of milk and whey, the bounce and give of the curds and the taste, aroma and texture of ageing and ripened cheese. Reading and using the recipes can give you a good foundation to start creating and using cheese, but it's being hands on, making it and the repetition that will enable your cheesemaking skills to grow.

Cheese paper and wraps

White mould cheese needs to be wrapped as it continues to ripen, helping protect the cheese while allowing it to breathe. Perforated cheese paper works well for this, as baking paper dries the cheese out and the cheese needs the right amount of moisture to continue ripening.

Cheese paper is available in specialty stores and online, and there are some available now that are plant-based, biodegradable and have reduced impact on the environment. Butcher's paper can also be used as a substitute, as can beeswax wraps, but can dry your cheese out.

Leaves such as fig, sycamore, chestnut and grapevine can also be used to wrap cheese. You could use any vegetable or fruit leaves so long as they aren't poisonous. That said, nettles also work, as in the case of Cornish Yarg – but wear gloves and blanch them to take the sting out before wrapping the cheese. Clean and blanch any leaves that you use quickly in boiling, lightly salted water and refresh them in iced water before patting them and drying. Remove any tough stems, then wrap and tie the cheeses and continue ageing. You can also soak the leaves in wine, cider, beer or spirit before wrapping to add another complexity to your cheese.

Brushes and rags

When rubbing, smearing, washing and brushing your cheese, use soft to medium brushes and rags. Cheesecloth works well, just make sure it's clean and roll or fold it up so you can use it to dip in brines and washes to smear cheese. Keep the cloths with the cheese in their containers and reuse them, washing as needed.

A soft to medium brush with natural bristles is good to help scruff up the rind and spread salt and bacteria on firmer aged cheeses to help develop the rinds further. This process is called 'morge' and is an important part of ageing some cheeses, such as Beaufort d'Alpage.

Cheese trier

Not a necessity, but if you plan to make more aged cheeses, it's a handy tool for checking on the progress of your cheeses as they age. This is a stainless-steel tool that takes a core sample of the cheese as it ages. Once the sample has been inspected, it is then put back into the cheese and plugged back up for the cheese to continue ageing.

Hooping the curds.

A note on measurements

When cheese is made in small quantities, the measurements are minute. I have already discussed measuring rennet in millilitres, cubic centimetres and drops on page 34. I use millilitres in the recipes in this book, but it's simple to convert to cubic centimetres (or cc) as 1 ml = 1 cc. Generally, 1 litre (34 fl oz/4 cups) of milk will be set with 0.25 ml (0.25 cc) of rennet, sometimes 0.2 ml (0.2 cc). One drop of rennet = 0.05 ml (0.05 cc), so you will need 5 drops to set 1 litre (34 fl oz/4 cups) of milk.

It is the same with starter cultures. Two to three grains can introduce enough microflora into that same amount of milk. I like to use the sterilised and dried tip of the thermometer to measure such small amounts – in the recipes I refer to this as a 'needle-tip amount'.

Some other useful notes on the recipes before you start

- Read the recipe in full before you start to grasp what you need to do.
- Ensure all your equipment is sterilised and keep it that way with boiling water (page 42).
- Have everything ready to go before you start, including your dechlorinated water for rennet (page 35).
- Check which rennet you are using and have the ratios calculated (page 35).
- Have your measurements for everything prepared.
- Make sure your thermometer is working and accurate.
- Check the ambient temperature of the room: around 18–20°C (64–68°F) is good. If it's too cool, warm it; if it's too warm, cool it – the milk needs to be at a constant temperature. Work during the day, as making cheese and fermenting at night is more challenging when the temperature is cooler.
- Ensure your work space is clean and tidy and you have everything in place.

Use clean hands to check the texture and temperature throughout the process.

Fresh cheese, creams, yoghurt and *butter*

I have often found that when you put the time, effort and resources into researching, sourcing good ingredients and making something yourself from scratch, the rewards far outweigh what money can buy.

It has been through many trials and tests that I have learned the basics of cheesemaking and, along with my background working in restaurants and being a chef, it has given me the unique opportunity to play around with cheese, curds, whey and the many by-products in the food I enjoy cooking and eating. It has shaped the way I see food and ingredients and further enhanced my appreciation of all things milky, funky and sour.

This chapter is all about fresher styles of cheese, yoghurt, cream and butter, of which there are many from different cultures and cuisines around the world, in particular from Europe and Asia where the rich histories of cheesemaking originate. These are the recipes that got me started and led to many different explorations in both sweet and savoury cooking, as you will find in the recipes later in Chapter 8. As they don't require special equipment or ageing, they are a good place to begin to learn the basics of cheesemaking.

With a high moisture content, most of these products have a limited shelf life and are best eaten as soon as possible. Making and enjoying cheese like this is quite unique, as these products are not readily available in supermarkets and you are able to play around with the texture and thickness. A large spoonful of just-made fresh white cheese (fromage blanc) is still one of my favourite things to eat — so simple and delicious.

I have not provided quantities for some of the flavourings, herbs and marinades, as I encourage you to experiment to suit your own palate. You will become more experienced with what works for you over time.

Fresh white cheese – fromage blanc

This was the first real fresh cheese I ever tasted, and I'll never forget it. It was so fresh, tangy, beautiful and delicate and like nothing I'd seen before in a kitchen or store in Australia. It was also the first cheese I learned to make and is still one of my favourites. In France, where this cheese style originates, it is a staple and quite readily available. It's like one of the 'mother sauces' in French cooking – so versatile and used as a base for many sweet and savoury applications, at breakfast, lunch or dinner. On its own, fresh and straight from the pot with a sprinkle of raw (demerara) sugar, it is one of life's greatest pleasures.

YIELD

Makes about 1 kg (2 lb 3 oz)

INGREDIENTS

2 litres (68 fl oz/8 cups) cow's milk
needle-tip amount (about 2–3 grains) of Flora Danica culture
0.5 ml (0.5 cc) rennet diluted in 5 ml (⅛ fl oz) boiled and cooled water – check manufacturer's label for dosage

EQUIPMENT

3 litre (3 quart) heavy-based stainless-steel pot
thermometer
ice
cheesecloth
colander/perforated tray for straining

METHOD

In a stainless-steel pot, gently warm the milk, stirring constantly and without scalding, to 85°C (185°F), then turn off the heat. Put a lid on the pot and let it sit for 30 minutes. If the milk does scald, start again.

Place the pot over an ice bath. While stirring, bring the milk down in temperature to 25°C (77°F).

Add the Flora Danica culture to the milk and allow to bloom for 1 minute. Stir for another minute, then put the lid back on and let it sit for 45 minutes.

Add the rennet, stir for another minute, then replace the lid. Leave the pot somewhere where it will not be disturbed and that is not too cool – around 20°C (68°F) – for 12–18 hours. (An ambient oven is good.)

The curd is ready when it is set and the whey starts to form a thin layer on top of the curd that smells deliciously lactic and tangy. Gently ladle the curds into a cheesecloth-lined colander or perforated tray to drain for a few hours, then refrigerate. (In kitchens this process is often referred to as 'hanging'.)

If you would like a thinner consistency, either add a little whey back into the curds or drain less. For a thicker curd, drain overnight or longer.

NOTE

Soft curd, drain for 4–8 hours Firmer curd, drain for 12–24 hours.

Persian feta, or marinated cheese

For most Australians living overseas, a jar of Vegemite brings on nostalgia, but for me it is seeing a jar of marinated Meredith goat's cheese with its familiar label. To my knowledge, this cheese was first created in 1984 by visionary Australian cheesemaker Richard Thomas, after he visited Iran and began marinating cheese in oil. In the short period since this fresh cheese was first made in Australia, it has become a mainstay of the Australian cheese industry with many dairies and cheesemakers now making and marinating their own styles, both here and abroad. There are two standout versions, both of which Richard had a hand in creating — Yarra Valley Persian feta, made with cow's milk, and the marinated goat's cheese from Meredith Dairy.

At the start of a meal, with fresh bread, olives, pickles and charcuterie, in a salad or vegetable dish or layered in a sandwich, this is a very delicious and handy cheese to have in the larder. There are now many varieties and flavours available on the market, including some with saffron and others made with sheep's or buffalo milk. For my version, I like to use a mix of cow's and goat's milk with confit garlic in the marinade. The goat's milk adds a nice sharpness, while the creaminess of the cow's milk gives a beautiful rich mouthfeel. I often play around with the marinated herbs and spices and the garlic cloves are delicious smeared on a piece of toast before topping with the cheese.

YIELD

Makes around 500 g (1 lb 2 oz)

INGREDIENTS

1 litre (34 fl oz/4 cups) cow's milk
1 litre (34 fl oz/4 cups) goat's milk
needle-tip amount (about 2–3 grains) of Flora Danica culture
0.5 ml (0.5 cc) rennet diluted in 5 ml (⅛ fl oz) boiled and cooled water — check manufacturer's label for dosage
sea salt flakes

MARINADE

200 ml (7 fl oz) oil (40% olive oil and 60% neutral oil like sunflower or similar)
½ teaspoon black peppercorns, blanched in boiling water for a minute (see notes)
thyme leaves — on the stalk is fine
bay leaves
lemon peel
garlic, blanched and confited (see notes)

EQUIPMENT

3 litre (3 quart) heavy-based stainless-steel pot
thermometer
ice
cheesecloth
colander/perforated tray or rectangular basket for straining
small weight of around 750 g (1 lb 11 oz)

Pressed curd

METHOD

In a stainless-steel pot, gently warm the milks, constantly stirring and without scalding, to 85°C (185°F), then turn off the heat. Put a lid on the pot and let it sit for 30 minutes.

Place the pot over an ice bath. While stirring, bring the milk down in temperature to 25°C (77°F).

Add the Flora Danica culture to the milk and allow it to bloom. Stir for 1 minute, then put the lid back on and let it sit for 45 minutes.

Add the rennet, stir for another minute, then replace the lid. Leave the pot somewhere where it will not be disturbed and that is not too cool — around 20°C (68°F) — overnight.

The next day, when the whey has started to form a thin layer on top of the curd, gently ladle the curds into a cheesecloth-lined colander or perforated tray to drain overnight in the refrigerator.

The next day take the curds out and weigh them in a large stainless-steel bowl. Add 2% of the weight in salt and whisk it in until you have a smooth and even consistency.

Line a flat perforated tray or rack with cheesecloth — enough to overhang and fold back on itself like wrapping a gift. Spoon the curd into the cloth and spread it out evenly. Completely wrap the curd in the cloth and press it down evenly with a 750 g (1 lb 11 oz) weight, then refrigerate overnight.

The next day, flip the parcel and place the weight back on top. Return to the refrigerator.

The third day, unwrap and move the curds around a little to allow more moisture to be pressed out. Press again with the weight.

For the marinade, gently warm the oil in a pan and drop the herbs, lemon and garlic in until the oil smells fragrant. Cool and set aside.

Flip the parcel every day until day 7 when it should have firmed up enough to cut and handle. Either cut into small squares or gently break apart and place in the cold oil to marinate. It can be eaten straight away but is best after a week of marinating. Make sure the cheese stays underneath the oil for best shelf life and store in the refrigerator.

NOTES

Boiling the peppercorns for a couple of minutes softens them and makes them edible with the cheese.

Cover the garlic cloves with a neutral oil and slowly bring to a simmer. Cook and confit them until soft, then cool and strain. You can use this oil as part of your marinade too.

Marinated cheese. Keep the oil and use to dip bread or in dressings.

Whole milk 'ricotta'

Ricotta means 'recooked' in Italian. It takes its name from the cooking process of reheating the sweet whey from a rennet-made cheese after it has acidified further, for the proteins left in the whey to form another curd mass. So, while this cheese isn't really 'ricotta' by definition, the name has stuck outside of Europe, and the process is very similar to a traditional ricotta.

As fresh whey is not readily accessible to most people, this cheese can be made this way quite easily at home and can be used in recipes that call for ricotta, although it does have a shorter shelf life due to a higher fat content.

This version is quite rich and fatty with the cream addition, so if you wanted something a bit lighter remove the cream and use all milk, skim milk or make the traditional whey version.

YIELD

Makes around 500 g (1 lb 2 oz)

INGREDIENTS

1.9 litres (64 fl oz) cow's, goat's or sheep's milk
100 ml (3½ fl oz) pouring (single/light) cream
pinch of sea salt flakes
45 ml (1½ fl oz) vinegar, diluted in 50 ml (1¾ fl oz) water

EQUIPMENT

3 litre (3 quart) heavy-based stainless-steel pot
thermometer
ricotta basket or colander/perforated tray for straining
cheesecloth

METHOD

In a stainless-steel pot, heat the milk, cream and salt, stirring, until the mixture reaches 88°C (190°F). Constantly stir to avoid catching – if the milk catches on the bottom of the pot it will burn and impart an acrid flavour in your cheese. If it starts to catch, change the pot before continuing.

While stirring vigorously, add the vinegar solution until you see flecks appear, then stir for a further 10 seconds and turn off the heat. Let it sit for 10 minutes.

Gently ladle the curds into a ricotta basket or cheesecloth-lined colander or perforated tray and strain for 15 minutes for a soft cheese, 30 minutes for a creamy but firm cheese, and 1 hour for a dry cheese. If the finished cheese is too thick you can thin it with a little of the whey or added milk.

The softer version, served warm and whipped with fresh bread, quality olive oil and aged balsamic vinegar, is a very good way to start a meal.

Clotted cream

Clotted cream originates from Devon, hence why it is often called Devonshire cream. It's delicious with a scone and jam, and whether you put it on before or after the jam is still up for serious discussion in Devon and Cornwall. You will need quality grass-fed cream for best results on this one – a good Jersey cream, as is traditional, works very well, as does Guernsey cream, which will give you a beautiful rich yellow cream. Use a wide, flat-bottomed ceramic casserole dish with a good surface area to caramelise it and give a good yield.

YIELD
Makes 350–400 g (12½–14 oz)

INGREDIENTS
600 ml (20½ fl oz) thick (double/heavy) cream

EQUIPMENT
dehydrator or oven
wide, flat-bottomed ceramic dish

METHOD
Preheat a dehydrator or oven to 80°C (176°F).

Pour the cream into a ceramic dish and place in the dehydrator or oven for 8–10 hours. After this time, you should see a yellow layer of caramelised cream skin has formed. This is the clotted cream. Take the dish out of the oven and chill in the refrigerator overnight to set.

The next day, scoop off the clotted cream and store refrigerated in an airtight container. You can use the left-over whey liquid to bake with in place of buttermilk and milk, especially for scones.

Cultured cream and créme fraîche

If you're lucky enough to have fresh raw cream available to you, simply leaving a jar of it on the kitchen bench will eventually sour into a beautiful tangy, thick cream. For those of us who don't have access to it, get the best possible, freshest grass-fed cream you can. Try your local farmer's market or boutique grocer. I like to use cultured cream for adding tang where recipes call for cream or for serving with desserts and cakes. For crème fraîche just use thick (double/heavy) cream instead to give a thicker-set cream.

YIELD
Makes 1 litre (34 fl oz/4 cups)

INGREDIENTS
1 litre (34 fl oz/4 cups) very fresh pouring (single/light) cream (see note)
needle-tip amount (about 2–3 grains) of Flora Danica culture or 1 tablespoon cultured buttermilk from previous batch

EQUIPMENT
2 litre (2 quart) heavy-based stainless-steel pot
thermometer
sterilised jar or bucket with lid

METHOD
In a stainless-steel pot, heat the cream to 25°C (81°F). Add the Flora Danica or buttermilk and stir for 1 minute. Pour into a sterilised glass jar or bucket with a lid, and let it sit in a warm place, around 20–25°C (68–77°F) for 24–36 hours.

After this time, it should have a lactic, sour smell and have thickened slightly. Place in the fridge overnight for it to thicken further.

When using it in recipes, whisk it slightly to loosen it to pouring consistency and use straight away. It can also be whipped to peaks and used in place of whipping cream.

Cultured butter – the cheesy one

A dear friend Casey McDonald once asked me about making a tangy, cheesy butter after he took over the running of a winery restaurant kitchen in New Zealand. He wanted something memorable to go with his potato focaccia at the start of the meal. After visiting Crown Finish Caves and seeing and tasting the butter they aged there for Momofuku Ko, I decided to play around with culturing cream with cheese and ageing butter in the wine cellars below the restaurant. The butter has been a big hit and, knowing Casey, I'm sure he's has been steadily improving it with every batch.

New Zealand is known to have some of the best dairy country in the world. The better quality your cream, the better quality your butter will be. A lot of supermarket creams aren't always grass-fed and are thickened with additives and thickeners, so they won't give you a really special end product. Good cream is expensive but for good butter it's worth it.

YIELD

Makes around 350–380 g (12½–13½ oz)

INGREDIENTS

1 litre (34 fl oz/4 cups) pouring (single/light) cream
50 ml (1¾ fl oz) cultured buttermilk (see notes) or a needle-tip amount (about 2–3 grains) of Flora Danica culture
small chunk of white mould cheese (for homemade see page 74) – about 25 g (1 oz) (see notes)
sea salt flakes

EQUIPMENT

2 litre (2 quart) heavy-based stainless-steel pot
thermometer
sterilised blender
fine sieve
sterilised bucket with lid (optional)
butter churn – or use a stand mixer
cheesecloth
colander/perforated tray for straining
ice
butter moulds
cheese cave

METHOD

In a stainless-steel pot, gently warm the cream to 28°C (82°F), then turn off the heat.

Using a sterilised blender, blend the tepid buttermilk and cheese together, then strain through a fine sieve into the cream. Keep the cream in the pot or in a bucket with a tight-fitting lid in a warm place and let it sit, covered, for 36 hours at around 20°C (68°F). Refrigerate for at least 24 hours.

In a butter churn or stand mixer, beat the cultured cream at low speed until the butter starts to form and the buttermilk separates. Keep an eye on the mixer while doing this as it will slosh everywhere and make quite a mess if you miss the separation. (After making butter a few times in the mixer, you'll start to recognise the sounds of when this transformation takes place. Until then, keep an eye on it.)

Drain the butter in a cheesecloth-lined colander or perforated tray and save the buttermilk for the next batch or any other recipe that calls for cultured buttermilk. (Just bear in mind that it will have a cheesiness to it.)

Wash the butter in ice water until the water runs clear, then squeeze it to remove as much moisture as possible – this helps prolong the life of the butter.

Weigh the finished butter and gently fold in 1% of its weight in salt, adding more if you'd like a saltier butter. You can now press the butter into moulds or roll it into a log.

If you happen to be ageing some white moulds or cheese, age the butter alongside it in your cave for 4–6 weeks. If not, it is still very delicious as is.

NOTES

You can use the buttermilk from a previous batch or a store-bought culture.

Goat's curd

Chèvre means 'female goat' in French – in Italian it's caprino and in Spanish it's cabra.

Chèvre can refer to any cheese made with goat's milk in France, especially in the Loire Valley. The cheeses can be in all sorts of textures, shapes, sizes, ages and flavours and can also be young or aged. They are not necessarily funky, not always soft, and can be quite seasonal. They are lactic-set cheeses, meaning they are made by the bacteria and lactic acid souring the milk into a curd without the addition of rennet. A steady and consistent temperature is required for this to occur, so the addition of rennet in this recipe allows for a quicker, more stable set curd and often a larger yield when draining. There is a recipe for a lactic-set chèvre curd on page 80 if you'd like to try it.

Homemade goat's curd is delicious, especially with cubes of raw marinated tuna on a crushed pea salad. You can start and end with the curd and use that for salads, vegetables, pastries or even make ice cream with it if you wish, or you can mould, salt and age it further. If goat's milk isn't your thing, try using half cow's milk – it will mellow it out a little.

YIELD

Makes 500–600 g (1 lb 2 oz–1 lb 5 oz)

INGREDIENTS

2 litres (68 fl oz/8 cups) goat's milk
needle-tip amount (about 2–3 grains) of Flora Danica culture
0.5 ml (0.5 cc) rennet diluted in 5 ml (⅛ fl oz) of boiled and cooled water – check manufacturer's label for dosage

EQUIPMENT

3 litre (3 quart) heavy-based stainless-steel pot or sterilised plastic bucket
thermometer
cheesecloth
colander or perforated tray

METHOD

In a stainless-steel pot or sterilised plastic bucket, gently warm the milk to 25°C (77°F). Add the Flora Danica culture and stir for 1 minute. Add the diluted rennet, stir for another minute, then replace the lid. Leave the pot somewhere warm (around 25°C/77°F), where it will not be disturbed.

After 12 hours, you should have a set curd with the whey starting to pool on top. If not, leave for another couple of hours until you do. Gently ladle the curds into a cheesecloth-lined colander or perforated tray and let it drain for a few hours. Refrigerate and use as soon as possible.

Goat's log

Softer styles of goat's cheese, particularly those from the Loire, come in all sorts of beautiful shapes and sizes: pyramids, rounds, cannonballs, squares, cylinders and logs. They are delicate cheeses and often rely on gravity and patience for them to drain and form their mass, density and shape. A log of chèvre is a simple, delicious and elegant way to make and serve cheese. Dust and roll with herbs, spices and flowers if you wish.

YIELD

Approximately 400 g (14 oz)

INGREDIENTS

- 2 litres (68 fl oz/8 cups) goat's milk
- needle-tip amount (about 2–3 grains) of Flora Danica culture
- 0.5 ml (0.5 cc) rennet diluted in 5 ml (⅛ fl oz) of boiled and cooled water – check manufacturer's label for dosage

EQUIPMENT

- 3 litre (3 quart) heavy-based stainless-steel pot or sterilised plastic bucket
- thermometer
- cheesecloth
- colander or perforated tray
- baking paper or cheesecloth

METHOD

Following the recipe for goat's curd on page 60, make the curd and drain for 24–48 hours at room temperature.

Once you have a firmer curd, roll into a log using cheesecloth or baking paper. Drain for another 24 hours at room temperature. Lightly salt the outside and refrigerate to use immediately. It can also be dusted with dried herbs, mushroom powder, ash, pepper or spice and aged in the refrigerator for a couple of days to dry out further. It's best eaten fresh.

Cream cheese

The best cream cheese in the world is bought by the pint and is actually found in New York City not Philadelphia. It's called Ben's cream cheese and, if you're going to have a bagel, this is what you'd want to schmear on it. Ben Gorodinsky originally created this unique cream cheese and other styles of fresh cheeses at Ben's Cheese Planet on the lower east side of Manhattan in the 1960s. Sometime in the early 70s he sold the business, and ever since Jonah Friedman took over, mystery has surrounded the processes behind this amazingly delicious smooth cheese, with the Ben's Cheese Planet website being perpetually 'under construction' for many years. Recently this has changed and they now have a website and other products added to the range. It's one thing to fall in love with the incredible texture of Ben's cream cheese but the story, secrecy and commitment to making something so delicious is what makes it so special. While this is not the famous recipe, this is how I like to make cream cheese. It's best eaten like Ben's — fresh and not kept for a long time. It can be whipped, softened and spread with buttermilk or milk to any texture that you like, as it will thicken slightly in the refrigerator. There are a couple of recipes in Chapter 8 that this recipe can be used for (see pages 136 and 192).

YIELD

Makes about 750 g (1 lb 11 oz)

INGREDIENTS

3.5 litres (118 fl oz/14 cups) full-cream (whole) cow's milk
500 ml (17 fl oz/2 cups) pouring (single/light) cream
100 ml (3½ fl oz) fresh lemon juice diluted in 100 ml (3½ fl oz) of water
100 ml (3½ fl oz) cultured buttermilk
sea salt flakes

EQUIPMENT

5 litre (5 quart) heavy-based stainless-steel pot
thermometer
cheesecloth
colander/perforated tray for straining
food processor

METHOD

In a stainless-steel pot, stirring constantly to prevent scalding, heat the milk and cream to 93°C (199°F).

While stirring, slowly pour in the lemon juice mixture until you see the milk curdle. Turn the heat off and let it sit for 5 minutes.

Ladle the curds into a cheesecloth-lined colander or perforated tray. Allow to cool for about 1–2 hours.

In a food processor, whiz the curds until you have a smooth, creamy cheese then, while whipping, add the buttermilk to soften. Season with salt and leave out at room temperature for an hour before refrigerating.

Either enjoy straight away or refrigerate and eat within a week. If it thickens too much, give it a whisk and thin with more buttermilk or whey as needed. Just remember, it's all about the freshness.

Cacioricotta curd

In late 2015, at the start of the southern summer, an eccentric and extremely passionate Italian natural wine importer, personality and friend by the name of Giorgio came to Melbourne to pour some delicious wines, dance in a convent and cook some beautiful things over coals. He wanted to serve heirloom tomatoes with green sauce and an Italian fresh cheese called cacioricotta. I had never heard of it so I looked into it.

From my reading, I learned that this beautiful cheese is from Puglia, and is quite a unique cheese in that it uses two cheesemaking techniques. 'Cacio' means cheese and 'cotta' means cooked and this cheese can be eaten fresh or aged and is usually made — depending on the region — with goat's or sheep's milk, or in combination with cow's milk. Eaten fresh, it has the sweet smell and taste of ricotta, and it is very good slathered on fresh bread with a little sprinkle of salt flakes, tomatoes and some quality olive oil. Aged, it is not too dissimilar from ricotta salata (see page 103), with the goat's milk flavour becoming more pronounced in a good way. It can be eaten as is or, as they do in Puglia, grated over pasta with orecchiette and tomatoes. (See Cacioricotta with tomatoes, anchovies and green sauce on page 144.)

YIELD
Makes about 500 g (1 lb 2 oz)

INGREDIENTS
1 litre (34 fl oz/4 cups) cow's milk
1 litre (34 fl oz/4 cups) goat's milk — if unavailable, substitute sheep's milk or use more cow's milk
0.5 ml (0.5 cc) rennet diluted in 5 ml (⅛ fl oz) boiled and cooled water — check manufacturer's label for dosage
sea salt flakes
sugar (optional)

EQUIPMENT
3 litre (3 quart) heavy-based stainless-steel pot
thermometer
ice
cheesecloth
colander/perforated tray for straining

METHOD
Warm the milks together in a stainless-steel pot with a pinch of salt, stirring so it doesn't scald, until the mixture reaches 85°C (185°F). Hold the milk at this temperature for 30 minutes.

Place the pot over an ice bath. While stirring, cool the milk to 40°C (104°F).

Once it's at 40°C (104°F), add the rennet, a drop at a time, and stir for a further 1 minute. Cover with a lid and let it sit undisturbed for 2–4 hours or until set (see note).

Gently scoop the curds into a cheesecloth-lined colander or perforated tray and strain for 4–24 hours depending on the consistency you'd like and the height and shape you drain in.

Season with a little salt — or sugar if you'd like a sweeter version.

NOTE
If using straight cow's milk, it may take longer to set, so be patient.

Pot-set thick yoghurt and labneh

If you enjoy yoghurt with your breakfast, make this. Serve it with raspberries, strawberries, blueberries, oats or honey. In fact, have it with anything you wish. It is so simple to make, very good for you, and once you've tried yoghurt you've made yourself, you probably won't go back to store-bought.

For your yoghurt cultures you can use store-bought yoghurt (see note), an older batch of yoghurt, or purchase yoghurt culture online or at health stores.

Labneh, or labne, is a yoghurt cheese with Middle Eastern origins and is made by straining yoghurt to remove the whey, giving a thicker yoghurt.

YIELD

Makes 1 kg (2 lb 3 oz)

INGREDIENTS

- 1 litre (34 fl oz/4 cups) milk of your choice
- needle-tip amount of Greek yoghurt culture, or 1 tablespoon store-bought Greek yoghurt (see note)

EQUIPMENT

- heavy-based stainless-steel pot large enough to hold the milk
- dehydrator or yoghurt maker (or use a low oven)
- ice
- sterilised jar or bucket with lid
- colander or perforated tray
- cheesecloth

METHOD

Gently heat the milk in a stainless-steel pot to 85°C (185°F), stirring to prevent the milk catching on the bottom.

While the milk is warming, preheat a dehydrator, yoghurt maker or oven to 40°C (104°F — don't use fan-forced).

When the milk reaches 85°C (185°F), turn the heat off, cover and leave for 30 minutes.

Place the pot over an ice bath. While stirring, bring the milk down in temperature to 40°C (104°F). Spoon the culture or yoghurt in and stir for 1 minute.

Pour the milk mix into a sterilised jar or bucket — or just use the pot if you wish — and cover tightly with a lid to place in the warm oven. Leave to culture for 8 hours, then turn the oven off. Remove the set yoghurt when cool. Refrigerate for 24 hours to allow it to set and firm up.

To make labneh, follow the instructions for the pot-set yoghurt above, then line a colander or perforated tray with cheesecloth and strain the yoghurt for 24 hours. Reserve the whey to use in other recipes. Whip the labneh if you would like a smoother consistency and store in the refrigerator.

NOTE

Often store-bought yoghurts have additives and thickeners to give them texture and firmness. If the yoghurt isn't thick enough for your liking, proceed with the labneh recipe.

Yoghurt cheese

Shanklish is a rich, dense, fudgy, crumbly, salty, spicy ball of air-dried yoghurt cheese, which can be broken apart and crumbled and is delicious served with vegetables, breads, eggs or salads. A cheese of Middle Eastern origin, it is actually quite complex to make using traditional methods. It is very fortunate there are cheesemakers in Australia and in other countries making it for sale in specialty stores.

This cheese, while not shanklish, is a way of preserving, marinating and spicing yoghurt in a similar way. It is a fresher cheese that is not dried out and therefore creamier and spreadable and delicious with warm flatbreads and honey. I really do recommend that you seek out and taste real shanklish too, though.

YIELD

Makes around 600 g (1 lb 5 oz)

INGREDIENTS

1 kg (2 lb 3 oz/4 cups) yoghurt
15 g (½ oz) sea salt flakes
200 ml (7 fl oz) 40:60 mix of olive oil and grapeseed or other neutral oil (see notes) – it may need more to cover the balls

SPICE MIX (SEE NOTES)

5 g (⅛ oz) cumin seeds
10 g (¼ oz) sesame seeds
3 g (¼ oz) Aleppo pepper
15 g (½ oz) sumac
5 g (⅛ oz) nigella seeds
4 g (⅛ oz) dried oregano

EQUIPMENT

cheesecloth
colander
sterilised jar

METHOD

Whip the yoghurt until smooth, season with the salt and drain in a cheesecloth-lined colander for 48 hours in the refrigerator. Pour and drain off the whey as often as needed, so the yoghurt isn't sitting in it. (The salt helps season the cheese and draw out more whey so, if you'd like a saltier, firmer cheese, add more salt.)

After 48 hours, you should have a more condensed curd, which is able to be rolled into small balls.

For the spice mix, in a small frying pan over medium heat, toast the cumin seeds by tossing them frequently until fragrant and toasty, then transfer to a bowl to cool. Repeat with the sesame seeds until golden but not brown, then cool. In a mortar and pestle or spice grinder, coarsely crush the cumin seeds and rub the sesame seeds with your hands to lightly crack them (see notes). Place in a bowl with the remaining spice mix ingredients and toss.

You can roll the curd balls by eye, or weigh them if you'd prefer uniformity, and drop them into the spice mix to cover, pressing the mix gently into them. Leave them to dry out and absorb the spices for a couple of hours before dropping them into the oil in a glass jar and sealing with a lid. It's best to let them marinate for a couple of weeks before using and keep refrigerated.

Use the oil in cooking, marinating or dressing as you use the cheese. Or you could strain it and use it for the next batch of yoghurt cheese.

NOTES

You can buy pre-made za'atar mix from Middle Eastern grocers if you'd prefer. Or try different spice mixes or adding colouring and flavouring with saffron or confit garlic.

It is best to do the toasting and mixing when you are spicing the yoghurt, but if you have made the mix earlier, lightly toast it again to release the aromas and freshen it up.

Aged and stretched *cheese*

Within the seven categories of cheese, there are thousands of different types made and enjoyed the world over. Many use the same methods, cultures, maturation techniques and tools to achieve varied outcomes, and some even fall in more than one category.

Learning the basics of fresh cheese, working clean, the timings, feel and temperatures sets the platform to progress into aged and stretched cheeses.

This chapter is about some of the basic 'recipes' that I have had success with in the home and commercial kitchen environments. Not all cheeses are covered here, as I wanted the book to give you an understanding of cheese, making cheese, and cooking with it. That is where real my passion lies — These cheeses can be used in the recipes in the following chapters.

You will need a small cheese cave for the aged ones (see page 43).

White mould cheese

There is something pretty special about making white mould cheese, then enjoying it with friends and family. White mould cheeses were the first aged styles that I made at home. They are a good step up from fresh cheese into the world of affinage.

When making these cheeses you will need to pay close attention to them, looking after them daily, to make sure the environment is right and everything is working.

These kinds of cheese ripen from the outside in, with the mould slowly growing on the outside. If they are aged for too short a time or at too low a temperature, you will have a chalkier texture; if you age them too long they will be oozy and may develop an unpleasant bitterness; and if they are aged too quickly they will droop, with the outer ripening quicker than the centre.

Although a fun process, making white mould cheese is not an easy skill to just pick up. Be patient, document what you are doing and keep refining your affinage skills.

A very ripe cheese.

White mould, soft cheese

Camembert, a style of semi-soft white mould-ripened cheese, is one of the world's most instantly recognisable cheeses. It is also often one of the most copied. True camembert, according to the purists, is made in Normandy, France (Camembert de Normandie) with mostly raw milk from the Normande breed of cow. The curds are not cut so as to retain more moisture and must be hand-ladled into the small round moulds. The cheese has been made in a certain way for hundreds of years by artisans in Normandy. Now, I've eaten some very good white mould cheese in places around the world too and they can reflect the herd, time and place they were made. Using this recipe, you can make your own white mould cheese too. Just don't call it camembert – call it yours.

YIELD

Makes 5 small cheeses

INGREDIENTS

- 5 litres (169 fl oz) fresh, unhomogenised, homogenised or skim milk
- 1.25 ml (1.25 cc) rennet diluted in 12.5 ml (¼ fl oz) boiled and cooled water – check manufacturer's label for dosage
- needle-tip amount (about 2–3 grains) of Flora Danica culture
- needle-tip amount of *Penicillium candidum* or white mould culture

EQUIPMENT

- sterilised plastic bucket or 7 litre (7 quart) heavy-based stainless-steel pot
- thermometer
- 3 ml (3 cc) syringe
- 1–2 × 3.5 litre (3½ quart) plastic boxes with hole in lids
- rack
- 5 small baskets or moulds – 8 cm (3¼ in) in diameter or similar
- clean towels
- cheese cave around 10–13°C (50–55°F)
- perforated cheese wrap or butcher's paper

METHOD

Using a sterilised bucket in a sink of warm water, heat the milk to 37–39°C (99–102°F), stirring from the bottom up to circulate the milk while heating. Alternatively, gently warm the milk in a stainless-steel pot on the stove to the same temperature, stirring to prevent scalding.

Sprinkle the cultures over the top of the milk and let it sit for a minute to hydrate, then stir for another minute and cover with a lid. Let it sit for 1 hour, maintaining the same temperature. This is the ripening stage.

After an hour, use a syringe to distribute the rennet over the surface of the milk and stir from the bottom up again for 1 minute. Place the lid back on and leave to sit undisturbed at the maintained temperature for 45 minutes.

Test for a clean break by making a small cut in the milk and sliding either your finger or knife at a 45-degree angle. If the whey runs into the crack, then you have a clean break. If not, allow for another 5 minutes and try again.

Using a knife, cut the curd into 4 cm (1½ in) squares and let it sit for 5 minutes.

A clean break.

Stirring the curds.

Using a curd knife, cut the curd horizontally, vertically and laterally into 4 cm (1½ in) squares.

Stir the curds every 5 minutes for the next 25 minutes.

Place the moulds in your boxes with a rack in the bottom and pour boiling water over everything to sterilise it all, then drain the water out.

After the final stir, when the curds are able to lightly bounce without breaking in your hand, gently ladle them into the baskets and begin to drain. Allow to drain for 30 minutes. As the curds settle, the whey will continue to drain so ensure they are not sitting in the whey and drain the container as required. Keep the reserved whey for use elsewhere if you wish.

After 30 minutes invert the baskets and flip the knitted curds. Be gentle as the curds will be very delicate at this stage.

Invert again in this same way after 1 hour, and then again 2 hours after that, removing the whey each time. Cover the boxes with clean towels and leave overnight to settle at around 20°C (68°F).

The next morning, invert the fresh cheese onto the rack and salt each one, about a teaspoon (c. 2% of its weight) of salt per cheese, covering them on all sides. Wipe out the container before putting them back in and allow them to dry out overnight, in a place around 20°C (68°F).

The next day, turn the cheese over. Clean out the container, making sure the rack isn't too wet, then put back for another night. This is drawing out whey and moisture, drying out the cheese and encouraging the bacterial growth to form a rind.

Flipping the cheese in the baskets.

Dry salting.

On the third day you should see some mould growth. Turn and place in the cheese cave to slow the growth down. You will need to turn them every second day for the next 2 weeks, cleaning and drying the container as the moisture builds up. If there isn't enough moisture and the cheese feels a little dry, add a small amount of water, or place a clean, damp cloth in the bottom. If it's too damp, dry out the container out and leave the lid askew for a day.

Flip the cheese every second day for 2 weeks, after which the cheese should be fully covered in beautiful white mould and ready to wrap to finish ageing. You will need to keep an eye on them and rotate them so they don't stick the rack/mat.

Take each cheese and wrap in special perforated cheese wrap, butcher's paper (or even washed leaves). Put the cheese back in the cleaned container and continue to ripen in the fridge or cheese cave, flipping the cheese every second day for another 2 weeks.

After this time, depending on the size of each cheese, they should feel slightly firm but engorged with a creamy and delicate centre. This is when the cheese is ripe and best eaten.

It will take practice and time for you to know when the time is right to cut open your cheese. However, it is good to play around with the ageing times and temperatures until you find out how you like your cheese. A shorter ripening will give a firmer cheese, while a longer maturation will give ooze and spreadability.

The important thing to remember is that this cheese is 'yours', so age it how you like.

Kimcheese

When I was working at Flora Bar in New York, we had a chicken dish on the menu that used the stem of bok choy (pak choy) only. We had so many leaves and stem-tops left over that one of the cooks, Joey, turned it into his mum's kimchi for staff meals. It was so delicious that I tried drying some out in a dehydrator. For the amount that goes in, a very small yield is returned, but it does pack a punch. Kimchi, with all that fermented goodness, flavour, saltiness and heat, is very good as it is, but when dehydrated it can impart so much flavour.

Drying out chillies, vegetables or fruits after fermenting/pickling them, or using the scrap from a milled sauce, can yield some pretty interesting powders and seasonings to boost flavour and umami in dishes and food too. I've had a lot of fun and success combining various ingredients with cheese over the years, and if you've ever had a kimchi and cheese toasted sandwich, you'll know that it just makes sense. Fermented milk + fermented food works.

YIELD

1 litre (34 fl oz/4 cups) milk will yield 1 small cheese

INGREDIENTS

white mould soft cheese (for homemade see page 74)
kimchi (see notes)

EQUIPMENT

dehydrator or low oven
blender, spice grinder or mortar and pestle

METHOD

Take the kimchi and evenly lay it out on dehydrator trays or racks, then place in a dehydrator or low oven at around 80°C (176°F) for 12 hours or until completely dry. Reserve any kimchi juice for later use — it's really delicious served in a tonic, as a seasoning for tomatoes, in a dressing or in a bloody Mary.

Once the dried kimchi has cooled down, process in a blender, spice grinder or mortar and pestle until a fine powder. You can sieve it if you'd like it finer.

When you have made the cheese, following the instructions for white mould soft cheese and are up to the stage of mould growth (around day four), lightly dust the cheese with the powdered kimchi. Be quite restrained with it — remember how much kimchi you started with and how strong the flavours are.

Continue to age the cheese, flipping every second day until it is ready to wrap to finish ripening. It is very good in a toasted sandwich or on its own.

NOTES

You could use sauerkraut, or any other fermented vegetable and it's always best to use something you've fermented yourself so you know what is in it. Dried mushroom powder, seaweed, used and dried coffee grounds, or dried mandarin and citrus peels are also quite unique and delicious to substitute in place of kimchi.

Goat's cheese – a wrinkly one

The beautiful, famed cheeses of the Loire in France come in so many shapes, sizes, colours and patterns. Many are made by lactic-set – meaning the slow souring of the milk is what coagulates the cheese with a minute addition of rennet. They tend to be more acidic cheeses and can be eaten at any stage of the process, fresh from the initial set as a chèvre curd, drained from the whey, or salted and aged for days to weeks. The *Geotrichum* mould is what gives these cheese the beautiful wrinkles and ripples that they are often associated with.

YIELD

1 small pyramid or two small round cheeses – depending on your basket size

INGREDIENTS

2 litres (68 fl oz/8 cups) goat's milk – it needs be fresh and quality
needle-tip amount of *Geotrichum candidum*
needle-tip amount (about 2–3 grains) of Flora Danica culture
0.05 ml (0.05 cc) rennet diluted in 12.5 ml (¼ fl oz) boiled and cooled water – check manufacturer's label for dosage
sea salt flakes

EQUIPMENT

3 litre (3 quart) heavy-based stainless-steel pot or plastic bucket
thermometer
cheese basket – 1 × small pyramid, or 2 small round baskets about 8–10 cm (3¼–4 in) in diameter
3.5 litre (3½ quart) plastic box with hole in lid
rack
cheese cave around 10–13°C (50–55°F)

METHOD

In a stainless-steel pot or plastic bucket, warm the goat's milk to 25°C (77°F).

Sprinkle the cultures over the top of the milk and allow to bloom for 1 minute, then stir for another minute. Cover, and let it sit, holding the temperature for 45 minutes.

Add the diluted rennet and stir for another minute, then cover and leave to sit undisturbed for anywhere from 18–48 hours, depending on the temperature of the room. It may take longer if the temperature is cooler or less time if the temperature is warmer. An oven or dehydrator that is not turned on can be a good incubator, as the temperature needs to stay as consistent as possible and temperatures drop at night. The milk needs to sit at 18–22°C (64–72°F) for the bacteria to slowly acidify and coagulate the milk into a curd.

When the curd has settled and there is a thin layer of whey on top, gently ladle the curds into the basket to drain. Allow to drain and keep topping up as needed. Don't be tempted to use another basket – the curds will drop as they drain and there is no need to flip them.

Allow them to drain for 24 hours at room temperature, demould, then salt all sides except the top and place on a rack to dry out for a further 24 hours, again at room temperature, in the box with breather hole open.

Once you see the mould growth blooming, place them into a cheese cave at 10–13°C (50–55°F) and high (90%) humidity. This can be achieved with the breather hole open in the tub and a small amount of water in the base. There is no need to flip the cheese, but do rotate it often so the base does not stick to the rack/mat.

Age them for 2–4 weeks depending on size and shape.

Pasta filata – spun paste or stretchy cheese

I'm not going to lie. (Or stretch.) Mozzarella, fior di latte, burrata, bocconcini, oaxaca and most types of stretchy curds are not part of my cheesemaking forte. I do enjoy eating them though.

Just after moving to Melbourne, I tasted my first handmade burrata – a luscious ball of creamy cheese served with grilled bread, fresh figs and aged balsamic. It was glorious.

Burrata and stracciatella came about in the 1920s as a way for cheesemakers in Puglia, Italy to use up all the scraps and trimmings from the daily mozzarella production with the curd trimmings hand-torn, folded with the cream taken from the day's milk, then placed into a stretched mozzarella 'purse'. Cheesemakers are very good at figuring out problems, waste solutions and how to make something from nothing. A hundred years later, burrata is now considered a high-end cheese and food product, with a price to match.

When I visited San Francisco in 2015, I missed out on seeing Luke Burgess make this style of cheese at a cooking class that was being held back in Melbourne at Cutler & Co.

I was lucky to get a copy of the recipe for the cheese curds and have since messed with them many times, sharing various iterations with other chefs who share a similar passion for cheese. Having never tried Luke's original recipe, I often wonder how this version would stack up against his. It's good with tomatoes, figs, garlic toast, pickles, beetroot (beets), greens, quality olive oil, salt and just about anything that you would have stracciatella or burrata with.

Traditional mozzarella, fior di latte and these stretched styles of pasta filata–style cheese are made by slowly acidifying and lowering the pH of the milk. This enables the curds to stretch, pull, thread and knot into cheese. It is the slow culturing and lactic acid from this process that gives mozzarella its flavour – adding acid to drop the pH for stretching doesn't allow for that lactic flavour to build up, which is crucial for a good mozzarella.

Interior of grilled cheese.

Baccarat

Quick mozzarella or Luke's curds

This isn't a traditional-style mozzarella curd with the citric acid responsible for the stretch. But with the addition of the lactic cream, this is just as addictive.

YIELD

Makes 500–600 g (1 lb 2 oz–1 lb 5 oz)

INGREDIENTS

- 4 litres (135 fl oz) chilled full-cream (whole) milk (unhomogenised) – it's best to use the freshest raw or unhomogenised milk possible
- 1 teaspoon citric acid powder dissolved in 125 ml (4½ fl oz) boiled and cooled water
- 1 ml (1 cc) rennet diluted in 2 teaspoons boiled, cooled water – check manufacturer's label for dosage
- 150–250 g (5½–9 oz) cultured cream (for homemade see page 56) or loosened crème fraîche (for homemade see page 56) (see note)
- sea salt flakes

EQUIPMENT

- 5 litre (5 quart) heavy-based stainless-steel pot
- thermometer
- cheesecloth
- colander or perforated tray
- slotted spoon
- small stainless-steel bowl

METHOD

Place the chilled milk into a stainless-steel pot and stir in the citric acid solution. The milk must be cold and not agitated too much or it will curdle

Over a gentle heat or in a water bath, warm to 28°C (82°F). Take care to not stir too vigorously, as this may cause the milk mixture to curdle and split. Once the desired temperature is met, maintain the temperature and gently stir in the rennet solution for 1 minute. Place a lid over the pot and allow to set for 15 minutes undisturbed.

Check for a clean break and cut into 5 cm (2 in) cubes, being careful not to break the curd up. If it's not set, wait for 5 minutes before cutting.

Place the pot back over a low heat or heat the bath and warm the curd slowly for 30 minutes, stirring gently every 5 minutes until it reaches 48–50°C (118–122°F). The curds should be quite firm and bouncy and hold their shape.

Once the curds are ready, remove from the heat. Scoop the curds onto a cheesecloth on a tray or colander and leave to drain and knit together for 1 hour. Warm a pot of water up to 70–75°C (158–167°F). Cut the firm curd in two and place in the hot water. You may need to put gloves on for this part. Scoop the curd mass out with a slotted spoon and begin to fold and pull the curds to stretch them a little, folding them on themselves as you go. Place the 'mozzarella' back onto the cheesecloth to drain. Rest at room temperature for a couple of hours.

In a stainless-steel bowl, gently whisk the cultured cream to achieve a smooth consistency, then whisk in the salt.

Gently tear and stretch the curds with your fingers and add to the cream, gently combining until you have what resembles rich cottage cheese. Season further if desired and store in the fridge. This is best eaten straight away.

If the creamed curds become too firm, leave them out for an hour and mix with some fresh cream to your desired consistency.

NOTE

If using crème fraîche, thin it out with fresh cream or milk before adding the cheese curds, otherwise it will set too firmly in the fridge.

A grilled cheese, but not haloumi

Some research suggests that pasta filata—style cheese, even though an Italian name, may have actually originated elsewhere — with Arabs introducing water buffalo to Sicily and Italy thousands of years ago. Along with Italy, spun-paste cheeses are made in the Middle East, Turkey and Greece, with arguably one of the most prominent — haloumi — hailing from the island of Cyprus.

Made with sheep's or goat's milk, this cheese can be grilled or served fresh. There are many recipes out there for 'haloumi', but there are also many stipulations and traditions around its production. Using cow's milk will make the cheese 'squeak', which isn't necessarily a bad thing. I do recommend you try with sheep's or goat's milk, but as they are more expensive and harder to find than cow's milk, blending might be an option.

YIELD

Makes about 600 g (1 lb 5 oz)

INGREDIENTS

4 litres (135 fl oz/16 cups) cow's, sheep's or goat's milk
1 ml (1 cc) rennet diluted in 10 ml (¼ fl oz) boiled and cooled water — check manufacturer's label for dosage

EQUIPMENT

5 litre (5 quart) heavy-based stainless-steel pot
thermometer
cheesecloth
large rectangular or square basket, or a few smaller ones (a round one will also suffice)
racks
1 kg (2 lb 3 oz) weight

METHOD

Warm the milk in a stainless-steel pot to 34°C (93°F). Add the diluted rennet and stir for 1 minute.

Maintain the temperature and check for a clean break after 1 hour. If not ready, wait for another 5 minutes and check again.

Cut into 5 cm (2 in) squares and let stand for 5 minutes. Cut again into 2 cm (¾ in) cubes and stir.

Over the next 45 minutes, stirring frequently, slowly increase the heat until it reaches 40°C (104°F).

Remove the curd gently into a cheesecloth-lined basket and gently press with a 1 kg (2 lb 3 oz) weight, flipping after an hour and then again after another hour.

While the cheese is firming up, heat the whey back up to 85°C (185°F) and cut the curd block into even-sized pieces, depending on the shape of your basket. Place the pieces back into the hot whey and, maintaining the temperature, cook them until they all float, about 30—40 minutes.

Lay the cheese onto racks and lightly sprinkle each piece with salt. Let stand until cool or overnight.

Using the whey or water, making a 8% brine (1.5 litres/135 fl oz/6 cups of water:120 g/4½ oz salt) and submerge the cheese in the cool brine to keep refrigerated. Because of the high salinity this cheese has a long shelf life and will keep submerged like this for a month If the cheese is too salty, next time you make it, reduce the amount of salt and soak the cheese in fresh water to draw some salt out before cooking.

Washed-rind cheese

Although these cheeses have their own category, they mostly originate from other styles — white mould, semi-soft, semi-hard, and some hard cheeses can also be washed-rinds. However, it is the softer, fudge-like and more pungent varieties that pick up the most characteristics from this ageing technique.

While white mould cheeses are matured with *Penicillium* and *Geotrichum*, it is the *Brevibacterium linens* bacteria that is required to be more dominant on the surfaces of washed-rind cheeses. Brevi, as it is abbreviated to, produces the reddish, orangey yellow and brown moulds found on those really stinky cheeses like Époisses, Soumantrain and other brightly coloured delights such as Langres.

Brevi bacteria love moisture and salt. Washed-rind cheese needs constant washing to help the brevi establish, grow and thrive on the surface of the cheese. At the risk of grossing you out, brevi is also the mould found between your toes and on feet — smelly cheese smells like smelly feet. Makes sense. Whereas we wash our feet to eliminate the mould and smell, cheesemakers wash their cheese with brine, alcohol and other solutions to encourage this bacterial growth to slowly break down the cheese as it ripens.

When making the brine to wash, use the whey as the liquid to dilute the salt — it has the good bacteria already in it and tap water can affect the mould growth A good brine solution is about 1–2% salt to whey, or beer, wine or cider; if you're using heavier alcohols such as spirits, dilute the spirit first with four parts liquid (whey or water) to one part spirit. Steer away from mass produced and sulphite-added beverages, as they can also affect bacterial growth. The more natural beers, wines and ciders can impart more interesting characteristics and they are also delicious to pair with your creations.

The gooey paste of a washed-rind cheese.

A semi-soft washed cheese

YIELD

Makes 2–4 cheeses

INGREDIENTS

4 litres (135 fl oz) milk
needle-tip amount of *Brevibacterium linens*
needle-tip amount of *Penicillium candidum*
needle-tip amount (about 2–3 grains) of Flora Danica culture
1 ml (1 cc) rennet diluted in 10 ml (¼ fl oz) boiled and cooled water – check manufacturer's label for dosage
a small piece of rind from a previous batch or store-bought washed-rind cheese
quality beer, cider or wine – see page 90 if using spirits as a wash

EQUIPMENT

plastic bucket or 5 litre (5 quart) heavy-based stainless-steel pot
small pot of boiling water
thermometer
1 ml (1 cc) syringe
2-4 small cheese hoops, about 8–12 cm (3¼–4 in) in diameter, or 12 × 8 cm (4¾ × 3¼ in) if rectangular
1–2 × 3.5 litre (3½ quart) plastic boxes with a hole in lids
cheese cave around 10–13°C (50–55°F) and 90–95% humidity
plastic rack or bamboo mat

METHOD

In a bucket in a sink of warm water, or alternatively in a pot on the stove, gently warm the milk to 38°C (100°F).

Add the cultures to the surface of the milk and allow to bloom for a minute, then stir for a further minute. Leave undisturbed for 45 minutes.

Add the rennet and stir from the bottom up for 1 minute. Maintain the temperature and leave undisturbed for 45 minutes. Check for a clean break and cut into 4 cm (1½ in) cubes. If not set, allow a further 5 minutes.

After 5 minutes, cut into 2 cm (¾ in) cubes and gently stir. Stir regularly over the next 25 minutes, maintaining the temperature – the curd should feel a little like a rare-cooked steak. Mould the cheese in small round or rectangular hoops. Allow to drain for 30 minutes, then gently flip. Flip again at 1 hour, 2 hours and 4 hours.

Using the whey or your beer, cider or wine, make your brine solution at 4% – so 4 g (⅛ oz) of salt to 100 ml (3½ fl oz) liquid. Gently warming the whey or alcohol helps the salt to dissolve and saturate the brine. Keep it in the cheese cave with your cheese.

The next day, flip the cheese and lightly salt the entire cheese with roughly 1.5% of its weight in salt. Leave at a moderate room temperature on the bamboo mat or plastic rack in the container with the breather hole open. Flip them again in the evening. The next day, flip them twice again to continue drying out.

On the following day, the cheese should be dry and can then go into the cheese cave in the containers with a little water in the base. You want a good amount of humidity, around 90–95%. If the cheese is not dry, leave for another day.

Before putting the cheese in the cave, dip a small clean rag or piece of cheesecloth in the prepared brine and smear it on the rind of a washed-rind cheese to extract some of the established moulds. Begin to wash your cheese by lightly rubbing the cloth and mould all over the cheese, except for the bottom. Place back in the container and then into the cheese cave. Do this every third day over the next 2–3 weeks, until you see the orange mould growing on the cheese. Make sure there is enough moisture in your containers and wipe them out occasionally.

Once the mould is established, it will continue to grow so you can stop washing your cheeses, but keep flipping them so the growth is even and they don't stick to the racks. They should be ready to eat 4–8 weeks after making them.

Semi-hard cheese

These styles encompass so many cheeses across the world. Comté, Gruyère, Reblochon, Manchego and provolone are all semi-hard cheeses, among the hundreds of varieties. For me, these cheeses are where raw milk, the environment and the craft of the cheesemaker and affineur really shines. They can be quite young at 2–3 months or aged for up to two years with the flavour, texture, appearance and profiles differing with each cheese.

Semi-hard cheeses are complex to make well, challenging to age, and make it even more difficult to coax those beautiful sweet, buttery, caramel notes, and fudge-like texture that, to me, a good cheese has.

During the cheese make, the curds are cooked and pressed allowing more whey and moisture to be removed. This lowers the water and moisture content and allows for them to be aged longer to develop their texture, flavour and characteristics. As they use a lot more milk in production, are aged longer and have less moisture, the sizes are generally larger to allow for them to age more slowly and evenly from the inside out. The wheel shape of these cheeses allows for the curds to be pressed and balanced evenly, gives a better shape and surface for mould growth, and, in days past, made it easier for the cheesemakers to roll the larger wheels to market.

Most of these styles are closely related, with small and often subtle variations in their cheesemaking methods. That said, I personally think there is no point trying to replicate some of these at home. The wheels are massive, each using around 600 litres (160 gallons) of raw spring/summer alpine herd milk, which allows for so much canvas for the cheese to develop, and you are never going to achieve that level of perfection at home.

That doesn't mean you shouldn't make and age semi-hard cheese though.

A tom, tomme, toma or tome is another style that is typically a round farmhouse style of cheese made in the Alps of Switzerland, France and Italy with cow's, sheep's or goat's milk by small producers, usually with milk from their farm. Smaller in size and more suited to home and farm cheesemaking, the milk as always, has to be quality.

Rinds of semi-hard cheese

Tom – a small semi-hard cheese

YIELD

1 cheese wheel, approximately 950 g–1.1 kg (2 lb 2 oz–2 lb 7 oz)

INGREDIENTS

10 litres (340 fl oz) milk of choice
2 needle-tip amounts (about 4–6 grains) of Flora Danica culture
2 needle-tip amounts of Type C starter
2 needle-tip amounts of PLA culture (see note)
2.5 ml (2.5 cc) rennet diluted in 25 ml (¾ fl oz) boiled and cooled water – check manufacturer's label for dosage
4 litres (135 fl oz) boiled water, cooled to around 60°C (140°F)

EQUIPMENT

12 litre (3 gallon) heavy-based stainless-steel pot or plastic bucket
thermometer
1 kg (2 lb 3 oz) hard cheese mould and follower or similar, so the curd can be weighted and pressed
3 ml (3 cc) syringe
5 small cheese hoops – about 8–10 cm (3¼–4 in) in diameter
cheesecloth
2 kg (4 lb 6 oz) weight
rack
3.5 litre (3½ quart) plastic box with hole in lid
cheese cave around 11–12°C (52–54°F) and 85–90% humidity
brush

METHOD

In a stainless-steel pot or bucket, bring the milk to 32–33°C (90–91°F).

Add the cultures and let them bloom on the surface for 1 minute, before stirring from the bottom up for a further minute. Cover the pot and leave the milk to ripen for 45 minutes, maintaining the temperature.

Add the rennet over the surface of the milk and stir in for a minute. Cover and leave undisturbed for 30 minutes, then check for a clean break. If not ready, leave and check again after 10 minutes.

With a knife, cut the curd into 5 cm (2 in) cubes, vertically and horizontally. Rest for 5 minutes.

Cut again into 2 cm (¾ in) cubes and gently stir. Rest for another 5 minutes.

Keep the milk at 32°C (90°F) for 40 minutes, stirring every 5 minutes. You can be more robust with your stirring of this cheese.

After this time, let the curds settle under the whey, then drain the whey off using a ladle until it is just covering the curd. Reserve the whey for later use.

Using the 60°C (140°F) water, slowly adding a small amount at time, bring the temperature of the curd up to 40°C (104°F) over the next 40–50 minutes, constantly stirring with a paddle or whisk. It may not need all the water, but it needs to be added slowly over the time. By the end of the process the curd needs to be broken up into pieces, a little smaller than a pea, and it should spring back when gently squeezed. Ladle out the whey and let the curds settle for 5 minutes.

Brushing the rind with salt to encourage growth.

Place a large hoop lined with cheesecloth on top of the curd mass and flip it over to capture as much of the curd as possible. Any curd pieces left in the whey can be hand-shovelled into the basket. Fold the cheesecloth over the top. Place the lid or follower on top of the curd and, with the whole cheese submerged under the whey, press with approximately 2 kg (4 lb 6 oz) of weight for 30 minutes.

If the cheese is not fully submerged, add some of the reserved whey back in, ensuring the temperature remains at 40°C (104°F).

After 30 minutes, remove the cheese from the mould and cloth, flip, rewrap in the cloth and place back in the mould. Remove the whey and place the cheese and mould in a draining tray for the whey to run off. Press with 2 kg (4 lb 6 oz) of weight for 1 hour.

Flip and redress after 2 hours and then again at 4 hours with the same weight. Leave overnight.

The next day, take the cheese out of the mould, weigh it and rub the entire cheese with 2% of its weight in salt. Leave at room temperature overnight, covered with a cloth, on a rack. Alternatively, if you want to brine the cheese, do this instead of dry-salting at this stage with an 18% brine made with the reserved whey, for about 8 hours per kilogram (2 pounds) of cheese. Brining is more beneficial for larger cheeses in large tanks of brine used in commercial cheesemaking operations with space and temperature control. I would recommend dry-salting for your cheese at home.

Flip the next day and leave to dry out for at least 48 hours, flipping once in between. Once dry, place in on the mat or rack into the container with the breather hole open and into the cheese cave to start ripening.

Rub and gently brush the cheese with a small amount of dry salt every second day for a week and flip to encourage the rind and bacterial growth.

After the first week of salting, continue to flip and lightly rub down with a brush twice a week.

As the cheese ages the white mould growth will develop with the brushing, slowly changing the rind and darkening it as it matures. Age for between 2 and 6 months – a longer ageing should produce more flavour and complexity.

METHOD

PLA is a cheese culture that helps with aroma, texture and rind development. It is available online at the same place where you find other cheese cultures.

Where there's a will, there's a *whey*

When making cheese, or most things for that matter, there is always a by-product followed by another, and then most likely another. Zero waste is a very difficult thing to achieve in all walks of life — humans are essentially walking waste creators. Throughout the years of working with and experimenting with cheese and following chefs and others working in the reduced-waste field, I've wanted to do better with by-products and the waste created. This curiosity and having the time to create has led to some profound discoveries and some truly spectacular failures.

Cheesemakers around the world have been doing this for thousands of years. Ricotta, anari and mizithra are whey cheeses made with the whey remaining from the curd making, Prosciutto di Parma is made with pigs that are fed with the whey from Parmigiano-Reggiano production, farmhouse butter in the UK is produced with whey and, in Scandinavia, brunost — a family of brown cheese styles and spreads — is made from cooking and reducing whey with milk or cream.

Using whey is not new, and aside from turning it into powders and formulas or bathing in it, there are many interesting and delicious ways to use it in cooking and beverage making.

Once the milk has been turned into curds and the curd cheese is made, the ratios of whey left over can differ depending on the cheese style, curd yield and starting volume. From 2 litres (68 fl oz/8 cups) of milk, you could expect around 1 litre (34 fl oz/4 cups) of whey, but this varies between milks, seasons, cheeses and makes.

There are two varieties of whey — sweet whey and acid whey. Sweet whey is made with rennet-set cheese, while acid or sour whey is made either by a slow acidification of the milk with no rennet, as in the case of yoghurt, or faster as with a quick mozzarella (see page 85), where acid is added. Naturally, a big difference is their pH levels, with the acidic whey having a lower acidic pH than sweet whey. This impacts the flavour and properties of each whey, meaning that not all whey is the same. This should be considered when using it.

Whey ricotta

As mentioned earlier in the fresh cheese chapter, ricotta means 'recooked' in Italian and is made by extracting the albumin proteins in the sweet whey left over from rennet cheesemaking. This traditional method results in lighter, fluffier cheese than when made with whole milk.

Traditionally, sweet whey is soured further and heated to a high heat to naturally curdle again, then left to bond together before being scooped out and drained.

Just like cheese, there are different methods for making ricotta. It can be made slowly, like above, or in a quicker way by adding acid to speed things up. Anari, made from goat's and sheep's milk from haloumi production in Cyprus, is made in a similar way to traditional ricotta with more milk added to boost the protein in the whey and therefore the yield.

This recipe is the quicker version, and a bit more acidic than a traditional ricotta, due to the addition of a curdling agent.

YIELD

Makes 250 g (9 oz), but it may vary

INGREDIENTS

2.5 litres (85 fl oz) sweet whey (from rennet-set cheese) — any less and the yield is too low, in which case you can add 250 ml (8½ fl oz/1 cup) milk to your whey as you are heating it up (you will need to stir it more often now, because of the risk of the milk burning, though) — check manufacturer's label for dosage
40 ml (1¼ fl oz) white vinegar, fresh lemon juice or a pinch of citric acid diluted in 80 ml (2½ fl oz/⅓ cup) water
sea salt flakes

EQUIPMENT

4 litre (4 quart) heavy-based stainless-steel pot
thermometer
skimmer
ricotta basket or similar, to drain

METHOD

In a stainless-steel pot, warm the whey over medium to high heat (add the milk to the whey as it reaches 40°C/104°F, if adding, and stir).

When the whey reaches around 93°C (200°F), or when protein lumps in the whey start to form, stir in the acid solution until larger flecks of curd start to form and turn the heat off.

If you want a sweeter, more traditional ricotta, leave the sweet whey to further ferment at room temperature for 12–24 hours. Make it in the same method, without the need for the milk and acid additions to curdle the whey. It should be acidic enough to curdle naturally when heated.

Let it sit for 10 minutes, then gently skim or ladle the curds off into a ricotta cheese basket or cheesecloth-lined colander. Let cool, then season with salt.

Taken like this and whipped with a whisk while still warm, will result in a very light, fluffy ricotta that is very good with bread, olive oil and balsamic.

Once cooled, it can be stored in the refrigerator in an airtight container for up to a week.

Salted ricotta – ricotta salata

Using the Whey ricotta recipe (opposite), follow the steps and, while the cheese is still warm, salt the curds, mixing through thoroughly.

Prepare a cheese basket with medium to larger holes, lined with cheesecloth and a 2 kg (4 lb 6 oz) weight to press. The mould should be high and shorter in diameter as opposed to a larger, flatter one, due to the cheese requiring pressing. Fill the mould with the ricotta and press with the weight for an hour at room temperature. After the hour, unmould, unwrap and flip the cheese, then wrap and press again for 24 hours at room temperature.

The next day, place on a perforated tray and lightly salt each side before refrigerating. Do this every day for 7 days, then age for a further week. Grate the cheese over summer vegetables, braises and pastas.

It will last about 2 weeks refrigerated and can be cryovaced to last longer.

Fermenting with whey

Lacto-ferment

Lacto fermentation is the process in which natural sugars found in foods are broken down by good bacteria called *Lactobacillus* to form lactic acid. It is done to safely preserve and add flavour, with kimchi, sauerkraut, sourdough, gherkins (dill pickles), kefir and yoghurt being examples of lacto-fermented foods.

It can be done naturally, in a brine solution, or with the addition of a starter culture, such as the mother in a sourdough, or cultures in cheese.

Fermenting with whey as a starter is a really simple way of fermenting more quickly due to the presence of lactic acid, sugars and good bacteria in the whey. Yoghurt whey is a good inoculator of ferments and, depending on the ambient temperature, can aid in fermenting things in just a few days — or even less in a warmer environment.

When soaking and fermenting grains, pulses, legumes or similar, adding whey helps to break down a nutrient-blocking antioxidant found in these foods, called phytic acid. Doing this increases the absorption of nutrients and aids digestion.

INGREDIENTS

whole raw grains, beans, nuts, seeds or rice
filtered water or boiled and cooled water — the chlorine in tap water can impede the fermentation
1 tablespoon whey

Burping a jar

This means to remove the sealed lids of a jar of fermented liquid for a short while, to enable the gas and air to escape. Reseal the lids after burping.

METHOD

In a glass jar, cover the grains completely with tepid water — about 20°C (68°F) — and add the tablespoon of whey. The grains will absorb the liquid, so make sure you have enough to keep them covered. Beans will swell to at least double their size so use plenty of water and a container large enough. Leave somewhere not too cool overnight until they have a slight fizz, ferment and a lactic aroma.

Strain, rinse, then cook as required. It's better to soak what you need at a time, but they will keep for a couple of days refrigerated, raw or cooked.

If fermenting nuts, you can dehydrate them after the soaking but cook them at a lower temperature, between 40 and 60°C (104 and 140°F), for longer to keep the good bacteria present. A higher temperature will kill off any bacteria you've introduced.

Lacto-fermented vegetables

Much the same as when pickling and preserving, use organic and the best possible quality fruit and vegetables, and wash and preserve them while fresh. Make sure they are submerged fully in the brine with a cabbage leaf or something similar placed on top to keep them submerged, as exposure to oxygen will cause them to mould. A salt brine is usually used but with the addition of whey. The process is sped up due to the presence of *Lactobacillus* bacteria in the whey. Always use non-reactive containers when brining, as they can rust and impart and impair the ferment. Ceramic pots are a good option.

For the brine ratio, it is taken from the volume of water so 2% of a litre (34 fl oz/4 cups), would be 20 g:1000 litres (¾ oz:265 gallons).

Fermented garlic

Cheesemaker extraordinaire Richard Thomas told me about this little trick and it is one of my favourite things to have in the fridge. When I was cooking in New York, it was all about layering the food and creating surprising elements. Green garlic juice was one of the ingredients that featured heavily – such a potent flavour. Fermenting garlic bulbs is a good way of not only preserving the bulbs for use, but the salty, briny, garlic liquid is a delicious source for adding salt and garlic subtleties to food with just a drop or two. It is a really powerful umami addition. The whole bulb can be sliced, diced or chopped and used in place of fresh garlic as needed.

INGREDIENTS

80 g (2¾ oz) whole garlic bulbs
tepid filtered water
3% salt
1 teaspoon whey

METHOD

Break the bulbs open and soak the cloves in tepid water for a few minutes – this helps loosen the skins and makes them easier to peel. Put the peeled cloves in a jar or vessel. Add enough water to cover, weighing just the water, then add 3% of that weight in salt, then the whey. For example, 100 ml (3½ fl oz) of water will need 3 g (⅒ oz) of salt. Completely submerge the cloves and cover with a torn cabbage leaf or baking paper. Leave to ferment for a week at room temperature or until fermented, burping the jar as needed. Keep in the brine in the refrigerator.

Fermented carrots with lavender

In 2019, a couple of friends from Paris, James and Shaun, came to New York to hang out and cook. James asked me to ferment a few things for the dinner and these carrots were included. I like to use whole baby carrots, but batons will also work and don't be shy with the lavender.

INGREDIENTS

baby carrots or carrot batons
filtered water
fresh lavender or seeds
2.5% salt
1 tablespoon whey

METHOD

Wash and clean the carrots and pack into a sterilised jar or container. Add water, salt, lavender and whey in the same way as the fermented garlic recipe (left). Submerge the carrots and cover to keep them submerged. Leave to ferment for 2–3 days, burping the jar a couple of times and refrigerate when ready. Cumin seeds, mustard seeds or rosemary are also delicious instead of lavender.

Fermented kohlrabi and dill

Peel the kohlrabi and cut into small wedges or batons, then do the same as for the carrots above, but substitute the lavender seeds with fresh dill or seeds.

Try other root vegetables and spice combinations but use the best-quality organic ingredients as possible – same with the salt and water. (The bacteria need nutrients to ferment and do not like chemicals.) If using vegetables that are higher in water content, you will need to increase the salt ratio to prevent them from going bad – dill cucumbers for example can require 5% salt in the brine. The lower the salt content the riskier the ferment can be.

Raspberry whey
Cherry soda
Pineapple soda

Whey cool soda

I love this, as do my nephews and niece. On a hot summer's day, a chilled passionfruit-flavoured soda is a really good idea. A red raspberry one for the kids might not be.

This is a fermented sparkling beverage, a bit like kombucha, a bit like water kefir, and when fermented well, spritzy, alive and delicious.

I've been fermenting whey into soda for a few years now, in both the Northern and Southern Hemispheres, in summer, autumn, winter and spring, and I can confidently say that you're going to have to work a bit for the fruits on this one. Find a suitable spot to keep them in your space, as they need a warmer spot to ferment well. In New York City, close to the radiator worked well in winter; in Sydney's winter it's a different story.

These ratios are what I have found to work well — but sometimes they can be too sweet, other times not sweet enough. Use this formula as a base and experiment with your own ratios and sweetness.

100% water — filtered, or boiled and cooled
50% fruit — organic is best
8–10% sugar — use raw (demerara), brown, coconut or honey
1.5% whey

So for example:

1 litre (34 fl oz/4 cups) water
500 g (1 lb 2 oz) pineapple
90 g (3 oz) sugar
1 tablespoon whey — yoghurt or fresh acid cheese whey, but sweet whey also works

METHOD

Put it all in a sterilised jar or fermenting vessel and give it a good shake. Leave to ferment for 2–3 days, checking on it and burping the jar as needed.

Once fizzy, strain the fruit out and ferment for another day or two before refrigerating. If it's not fizzy, leave it out for another day.

Use raw sugar and honey to get a good ferment — ones that have been treated may impede the fermentation and you may need to adjust the amounts as the fruit can be sweeter at certain times of the year.

Vinegar and pickles

Whey vinegar pickle

When buying herb bunches, especially tarragon and mint, there's always some that just sits in the bottom of the drawer, along with the stalks. With sweet whey from fromage blanc (fresh white cheese), you can make an infused vinegar pickle that can be used in sauces, dressings and seasonings. A mint pickle makes for a good sauce with Sunday roast lamb or a pea salad, a chilli one with melons, grilled cheese and tarragon with asparagus or in bearnaise (3 parts whey: 1.5 parts vinegar: 1 part sugar + pinch of sea salt flakes). It is also delicious when made with chilli or sliced ginger.

Mint/tarragon/chilli/ginger vinegar

INGREDIENTS

sprig/stems/leaves/chilli/peeled sliced ginger (see note)
150 ml (5 fl oz) whey
75 ml (2½ fl oz) white vinegar
50 g (1¾ oz) sugar
¼ teaspoon salt sea salt flakes

METHOD

Warm the liquid ingredients and pour over the stem, sprigs, bulbs or chilli.

Cool and then cover with an airtight lid and keep in the fridge for up to a month.

NOTE

I have left the amount blank as you may have less or lots. The warm pickle needs to cover what you are pickling and some things like chilli will need less as it can be quite spicy.

Pickled beetroot

An Australian dining table icon — sliced pickled beetroot. My wife Andrea's favourite.

INGREDIENTS

1 bunch of baby beetroot (beets) — about a squash ball or tennis ball size, washed — keep the stems and make the Beetroot marmalade (page 201)
150 ml (5 fl oz) whey
75 ml (2½ fl oz) white vinegar
50 g (1¾ oz) sugar
¼ teaspoon sea salt flakes
5 allspice berries
1 bay leaf

METHOD

Preheat the oven to 200°C (400°F). Spread the base of a baking tin with table salt and place the beetroot on top. Cover with foil and bake until they are just cooked, about 30–45 minutes, testing with skewer. They should still be firm but able to be peeled — you may need to use a small knife or peeler for this. Cool and then peel.

Make the pickle by warming the liquids and dissolving the sugar and salt in a small saucepan over low heat. Once dissolved, drop the allspice and bay leaf in and turn the heat off and let it sit.

Using a mandoline, thinly slice the beetroot then pour the warm pickling liquid over the top and set aside to cool. Once cool, refrigerate.

They are delicious with all sort of cheese, salads, and — contentiously — on a burger.

Whey sourdough

A whey sourdough loaf.

I must confess I am no baker, and I am certainly no food scientist, but since I've started learning and focusing on how to better balance life, work and other pursuits, I've been dabbling in breadmaking with whey.

As you'll notice, cheese produces a lot of whey and there's only so much you can use in various applications. Substitute the water for whey in your favourite bread recipe (I like Michael James's sourdough recipe from his book *The Tivoli Road Baker*), bearing in mind it will add lactose – but I'm sure if you've got this far, that isn't a concern.

Cheese whey crackers

This is a good way to use up whey and sourdough starter if you have them. If not, substitute water and dried yeast.

The crackers are good with cheese and dip and will keep for a week in an airtight container. Reheat them in the oven for a few minutes if stale.

YIELD

Serves 10–15, depending on size and thickness

INGREDIENTS

50 g (1¾ oz) sourdough starter or ½ teaspoon dried yeast
100 ml (3½ fl oz) whey or water at 30°C (86°F) – if using yeast, increase to 200 ml (7 fl oz)
140 g (5 oz) plain (all-purpose) flour
15 g (½ oz) rye flour – or malt if you'd like a darker cracker
pinch of sea salt flakes
pinch of sugar
whisked egg white or olive oil, for brushing

METHOD

Mix the starter or yeast with the whey or water and let it sit for 5 minutes.

Add the flours, salt and sugar and knead for 5 minutes. Let the dough rise for 30 minutes, then knead into a ball and place in a lightly greased bowl. Cover and refrigerate overnight.

The next day, preheat the oven to 180°C (350°F). Flour and roll the dough thin with a pasta roller or rolling pin. Lay the sheets on baking paper–lined trays, then prick them a few times with a fork before brushing them with egg white, olive oil or more whey and seasoning with sea salt flakes.

Bake for 7 minutes, then flip and bake for a further 5–6 minutes until golden.

Sheet music crackers

I once worked in one of those idyllic farm-to-table restaurants that turned out to be not so idyllic. I did meet a wonderful Belgian chef called Nina, though. She made the most beautiful carasau crackers with flowers from the kitchen garden to serve with cheese. Pane carasau are stiff and crackly flatbreads originating from Sardinia, where they are also known as carta de musica, which translates to 'sheet music' because of their thinness. When Nina would roll them out, with the flowers and leaves embedded through the long paper-thin sheets, you could see why. They are a traditional favourite of Sardinian sheepherders, where they are twice baked in hot oven with a yeasted dough to enjoy with pecorino.

YIELD
Makes 20+ serves, depending on size and thickness

INGREDIENTS
75 g (2¾ oz/½ cup) 00 flour
60 g (2 oz/½ cup) fine semolina, + extra for dusting
80 ml (2½ fl oz/⅓ cup) water
pinch of sea salt flakes
fresh flowers and herbs (optional)

METHOD
In a small bowl, mix the flours and salt, then add the water and knead until a smooth dough is formed. It will seem dry at first but work it to bring the dough together. Cover and refrigerate for an hour.

Preheat the oven to 200°C (400°F) and put a large flat baking tray in.

Cut the dough into quarters and, using a pasta machine, roll a dough ball through it, starting on a high setting down to the lowest, until paper thin. Put the dough through twice on the lowest setting, then flour it liberally with semolina to stop them sticking. Keep the other dough balls covered with a damp cloth while rolling them out so they don't dry out. You can also use a rolling pin; they should be paper thin as per the name, but a little thicker is okay.

Lay the sheets out and brush with olive oil and sea salt, then bake them on the preheated baking tray, like a pizza stone, for 4 minutes, then flip and rotate them, baking for a further 4–5 minutes until golden in colour. Once cooked, cool on a wire rack and continue cooking the rest.

If you want to add the flowers and herbs, add them at the first rolling stage. Roll the dough out to a long rectangle about 40–50 cm (16–20 in). Brush one half of the dough with water and lay the flowers and leaves down – they can be quite condensed as they will spread out after rolling. Trim any stems or buds because if they are not flat they can tear through the dough. Fold over the other half like a book and press down to stick. Cut the dough in half, then continue to roll out thin.

Store in an airtight container once cooled.

Parmesan stock

Keep your parmesan rinds in the freezer. If you don't have enough, sometimes cheesemongers sell them.

When I was at trade school, I made a pot of chicken stock for the first time at home. I strained out the broth and had the mirepoix sitting on the sink ready to be thrown in the trash, when Dad walked in and started snacking on the boiled mashed carrots and gnawing on the bones. I laughed at him then, but now think he was onto something as I would advise you to snack on those cheese rinds after the broth has been strained.

YIELD

Makes 1–1.2 litres (34–41 fl oz)

INGREDIENTS

olive oil
250 g (9 oz) parmesan rinds
100 ml (3½ fl oz) white wine
1.25 litres (42 fl oz/5 cups) water or sweet whey — acidic whey can be a bit intense and sour the stock, so if you do use it, use half whey and half water
small piece of kombu or a bay leaf (optional)
1 garlic clove, bruised with a knife
½ brown onion, roughly diced

METHOD

In a wide, heavy-based pot, add a splash of olive oil and sweat the onion and garlic until soft and translucent. Add the rinds and sweat for a couple of minutes until they start to caramelise, stirring so they don't stick to the bottom. If they catch and burn, they will impart a bitter flavour to the stock. Deglaze with the white wine and scrape off any cheese stuck to the pot.

Add the water/whey and kombu and bring to a simmer. Stir every so often, so the cheese doesn't stick to the bottom. Simmer for 1 hour to 90 minutes, then strain and cool. Straining the stock while it is warm stops the cheese rinds sticking to the bottom of the pot as it cools. Soak it and clean after straining so as not to end up with a stubborn cheese mess in the bottom of the pot. Refrigerate or freeze the stock once cool and use for soup, pasta and sauces.

Whey powder

If you've ever seen whey protein powder at health food stores and gyms, this is how it is made. The recipe doesn't make a lot, but a little goes a long way. It's delicious in a banana smoothie!

YIELD

Makes 70–100 g (2½–3½ oz)

INGREDIENTS

2 litres (68 fl oz/8 cups) whey

METHOD

Pour the whey into a glass baking dish or stainless-steel tray with a good amount of surface area so you can make a shallow pool. Place in a dehydrator or low oven at 100°C (212°F) for 12 hours or until the whey has dried into a sheet. Allow to cool and then, using a baker's card or fish/egg flip, scrape the sheet into a blender and blend into a powder. Store in an airtight container in a dark, cool place.

Buttermilk

No whey. Buttermilk is the by-product of butter production.

The cream is churned and when the solid butter is formed, the liquid that is left is called buttermilk. Cultured buttermilk is delicious in baking and many other applications and with more producers making cultured butter, proper buttermilk is becoming more available. It can even be used to make curd.

Buttermilk ricotta

YIELD
Makes 125–250 ml (4–8½ fl oz/½–1 cup)

INGREDIENTS
500 ml (17 fl oz/2 cups) cultured buttermilk
1 litre (34 fl oz/4 cups) unhomogenised milk

METHOD
Combine the buttermilk and milk in a stainless-steel pot and bring to 80–82°C (176–180°F), stirring often to prevent it from scorching. When it starts to form curds on top, turn off the heat and let sit for 20–30 minutes without stirring. The curds need to knit together and stirring it will drop your yield.

Gently ladle and skim the curds from the top into a cheesecloth-lined basket, drain and cool. Keep in the refrigerator for up to a week.

You can use the whey that is left in the pancake recipe (see page 120) or for other baking purposes.

Buttermilk curd

Using buttermilk that has been left to sit at room temperature for a few hours after churning can give you a delicious, sour, buttery curd, very similar in texture to a fresh white cheese curd. The flavour, however, is quite different – more lactic, buttery and tangy. If using store-bought buttermilk, you don't have to leave it out and can make it straight away.

METHOD
In a stainless-steel pot, slowly warm the buttermilk to 70–75°C (158–167°F). As it hits the temperature you should start to see the curds separating from the whey. Turn off the heat and let it sit for a minute.

Drain the curds into cheesecloth, wrap up and let hang over a bowl or sink for a couple of hours depending on the texture you'd like.

Take the curds from the cheesecloth, season with salt and refrigerate.

Microplane a small amount of fresh garlic and chop fresh dill into the mixture for a delicious dip to go with cucumbers or fried chicken, or as a base for ranch dressing.

Fromage blanc 2/10
Mayo 2/10
Blood orange 24/9

Dressings

Whey vinaigrette

A simple dressing for salad leaves, beetroot (beets), cucumbers or grains.

YIELD
Makes about 250 ml (8½ fl oz/1 cup)

INGREDIENTS
100 ml (7 fl oz) grapeseed oil
50 ml (3½ fl oz) extra-virgin olive oil
½–1 teaspoon raw honey
50 ml (3½ fl oz) sweet or acid whey
½ tablespoon chardonnay vinegar, to taste
sea salt flakes
freshly ground black pepper

METHOD
Blend the two oils together in a bowl. Whisk the honey, whey and vinegar together in another bowl. Slowly add the oil, whisking to emulsify. Season and serve.

Preserved lemon and honey whey vinaigrette

A sharp and sweet dressing that is quite thick and goes well with grains, salads, leaves, roasted vegetables or fish.

YIELD
Makes 220–390 ml (7½–10 fl oz)

INGREDIENTS
80 g (2¾ oz) preserved lemon, seeds removed
40 g (1½ oz) raw honey
80 ml (2½ fl oz/⅓ cup) whey
150–200 ml (5–7 fl oz) grapeseed or other neutral oil

METHOD
In an upright blender, blitz the lemon, honey and whey until smooth. Slowly add the oil and emulsify until thick. Check the seasoning – it shouldn't need salt because of the lemon but may need a touch more honey depending on your tastes. Keep refrigerated.

Dried apricot, honey and whey dressing

Prunes, peaches, plums and other dried fruits will also give you a delicious dressing, as will using maple syrup instead of honey. As this is made in a blender or Thermomix, don't halve the recipe as it may not be incorporate properly.

YIELD
Makes about 450 ml (15 fl oz)

INGREDIENTS
80 g (2¾ oz) dried apricots, soaked in warm water or whey for a day to fully rehydrate
40 g (1½ oz) honey
30 ml (1 fl oz) whey
275–325 ml (9½–11 fl oz) grapeseed oil
35 ml (1¼ fl oz) white balsamic vinegar
juice of ½ lemon

METHOD
Drain, the apricots then place in a bowl with the honey, whey and oil. Cool in the refrigerator.

In a blender or Thermomix, blend the apricots with the honey and whey until smooth, slowly adding the oil to emulsify until thick. Season with the vinegar, lemon juice and salt

If the emulsion gets too warm, it can split and separate, which is okay. Just put it in the refrigerator, cool it down and whisk it together again to emulsify. Keeps for up to 2 weeks in the refrigerator.

Whey-onnaise

Whey is a protein and can be used quite effectively as emulsifying agent when thickened slightly — a bit like an egg yolk. However, it doesn't have the richness that an egg yolk provides and is quite acidic in comparison.

A bowl of just-warm potato salad is a good use for this dressing, as are salad leaves. A little goes a long way!

YIELD

Makes 220–350 ml (7½–12 fl oz)

INGREDIENTS

500 ml (17 fl oz/2 cups) whey
200–300 ml (7–10 fl oz) blended oil
pinch of sea salt flakes

METHOD

In a saucepan over medium heat, reduce the whey by three-quarters or until syrup-like.

While the whey is warm, emulsify in a blender with the oil until thick, then season.

Real mayonnaise

Adding whey can extend the shelf life of homemade mayonnaise and other items, as the bacteria in the whey act as stabilisers and preservatives. It will not be shelf-stable like the jar stuff but will last longer than a regular homemade mayo. That said, a fresh, well-made mayo is always best, so don't make too much at a time and always check the seasoning, flavour and consistency before using.

When making mayo, gently warm and thicken the yolks and egg by whisking them for a few minutes before adding the oil and emulsifying. It not only gives a really silky texture but allows the oil to incorporate better and results in a more stable mayonnaise. If you are making it in a food processor, just whiz the eggs up until fluffy first.

YIELD

Makes about 500 g (1 lb 2 oz)

INGREDIENTS

2 egg yolks + 1 whole egg
350–450 ml (12–15 fl oz) grapeseed oil or other neutral oil — depends on your desired thickness
pinch of sea salt flakes
½ teaspoon fresh whey from yoghurt or fresh white cheese (for homemade see page 48), at room temperature

METHOD

In a food processor, whiz the egg yolks and egg for 3–4 minutes until light and fluffy, then slowly add the oil until emulsified and the desired thickness. Add the whey and season with salt.

Leave out for an hour before refrigerating to allow the lactic acid to do its thing.

A teaspoon of garlic brine also adds a nice element to your mayonnaise.

Whey caramel

Whey contains lactose. Lactose is a sugar and therefore caramelises when the whey is slowly cooked down. This takes a lot of time and energy but is worth it.

YIELD

Makes 125–180 ml (4–6 fl oz/½–¾ cup)

INGREDIENTS

2 litres (68 fl oz/8 cups) sweet whey
60–80 ml (2–2½ fl oz/¼–⅓ cup) pouring (single/light) cream

METHOD

Strain the whey through cheesecloth into a heavy-based, preferably wide, saucepan. Heat and begin to slowly reduce the whey, straining another three to four times throughout the reduction to remove any solids that will cause it to become grainy. When it has reduced by about three-quarters, add the cream and continue reducing. It will start to caramelise and brown. Process it in a blender and strain into a smaller, clean pot. Keep reducing until glossy and when at the required consistency, remove from the heat. It shouldn't be pourable when cool. Cool over a water bath, stirring frequently to prevent it crystallising. You can salt, spice or season it at this stage and then store in a refrigerator.

Whey and fat caramel

When we were kids, Nanna would always keep a crystal bowl of lollies on her living room table for us kids – Pascal Country Mints and Pascal Columbines, both of which have sadly been discontinued. Columbines were an intense chewy caramel, cut in a square shape and wrapped in pink and blue foil.

These little caramel bites remind me of those candies, and were first created when I was working at a winery that would get whole and half animals in to butcher. There was always a surplus of beef, pork or lamb fat. One day, when making some whey caramel, I added beef fat in place of butter to it, and it took on a deeply intense flavour. Softened with a little white chocolate, it was a very interesting and unusual bite. Duck fat and cod fat have also yielded interesting results, but you could also use butter if that is more to your palate. Keep it in the freezer and shave it over chocolate ice cream.

YIELD

Makes 300–450 g (10½ oz–1 lb)

INGREDIENTS

4–5 litres (135–169 fl oz) whey
40 g (1½ oz) thick (double/heavy) cream
20 g (¾ oz) rendered fat – beef, lamb, duck or cod or to taste
1 gold-strength gelatine leaf, bloomed in iced water
25 g (1 oz) Valrhona Ivoire 35% white chocolate or other quality white chocolate, melted

METHOD

Place the whey in a large stainless-steel pot, bring to a simmer and cook for several hours until it starts to thicken. As it warms, foam will start to appear – skim this off and reserve. Continue to reduce the whey slowly, and stir often as otherwise it can become grainy, until it reaches the consistency of a thin porridge and begins to caramelise.

At this point any reserved curds can be stirred back in. Add the cream and reduce for a further hour or so over low heat until like a caramel.

Add the fat, bloomed gelatine and melted white chocolate and mix in well.

Line a small tray with lightly greased baking paper.

Pass the caramel through a fine sieve into a bowl, then cool, stirring frequently, and set in the tray in the freezer.

Dice in small squares to serve and keep in an airtight container in the freezer.

Sourdough and buttermilk pancakes

Sourdough is another one of those things that creates waste – there's always that little bit of starter that is taken out to feed the mother and then there's the left-over stale crusts and end bits. For the adventurous, those stale pieces are gold mines for growing and harvesting natural blue mould cultures for cheesemaking and again, refer to David Asher's book (see page 216) for hints and tips there.

For the pancake lovers, keep your sourdough discard and your buttermilk.

My buddies Casey and Manu used to have a spot in Collingwood, Melbourne called Rockwell and Sons that made one of the greatest burgers I've ever had – the Double Patty Smash.

Casey is an American chef who worked at some of the NYC institutions, and Manu is a big-hearted, humble front-of-house/operations guy who knows everyone in the food world.

That place was my go-to after a big week in the city – always a big hug from Manu at the door followed by a beer and a shot, a Double Patty Smash, then many more beers at the bar.

Rockwell has since closed, but Casey and Manu have gone on to build some great spots in Melbourne and have always been such good friends and supporters.

Manu loves pancakes, Casey loves good beer and cooking with buttermilk, so this recipe reminds me of them and that special place.

You can make the batter a day ahead, then add the baking powder and bicarbonate of soda in the morning. Any batter left over will last overnight and still give a fluffy pancake.

YIELD

Makes 6–8 large pancakes

INGREDIENTS

150 g (5¼ oz) sourdough discard
2 large eggs
175 ml (6 fl oz) buttermilk or milk
50 g (1¾ oz) clarified butter + 125 g (9 oz)
140 g (5 oz) plain (all-purpose) flour
20 g (¾ oz) sugar
pinch of sea salt flakes
1 teaspoon baking powder
½ teaspoon bicarbonate of soda (baking soda)

METHOD

Whisk the sourdough discard, eggs, buttermilk, the 50 g (1¾ oz) of clarified butter, the flour, sugar and salt together – keep it a bit lumpy. Place in the refrigerator overnight.

The next morning, sift in the baking powder and bicarbonate of soda and whisk them through. Add a little more buttermilk if the batter is too thick.

In a large flat non-stick pan over medium–high, heat a good amount of the remaining clarified butter to almost shallow-fry the pancakes.

When the butter is hot, pour the batter into the pan using a 90 ml (3 fl oz) ladle, keeping a good amount of space between each pancake. Cook, adding more butter as needed, to keep them frying until bubbles appear in the middle and the outer edges brown heavily and crisp up. I like them very charred and crispy, but turn the heat down if you prefer a softer, golden crust. Flip and cook for another minute or so, then place them on a rack in a warm oven to keep them warm and continue cooking the rest.

Serve immediately with maple syrup, butter, buttermilk curd, lemon or whatever you enjoy your pancakes with. A beer and a shot perhaps.

Cooking with cheese and *dairy*

Cheese is so much more than just an after-dinner thing, and cheese and dairy play huge roles in cooking — when in doubt just add more butter, right?

French cooking is steeped in the use of butter (beurre) and cheese, but most of my experience and knowledge wasn't with using cheese in dishes and food outside the obligatory Parmigiano-Reggiano on pasta or salad, fresh goat's curd with beetroot (beets), or mozzarella with fresh tomatoes.

The cheeses used in the recipes in this chapter can be ones that you've made (using the recipes in this book), or they can be bought from a cheesemonger. They may be the exact varieties I mention, or you might want to experiment and use something different.

Some of the recipes may need more salt, more acid or more fat because when a recipe calls for cheese, it shouldn't be measured. You put that in with your heart.

These recipes have come about through my travels, experience, constant tasting and all the years of working with other great cooks. Some take inspiration from places I've worked, places I've travelled, people I've worked with, and cheeses that I've made and eaten.

Some of the recipes may be missing quantities for flavouring, marinades, garlic and seasonings, as I encourage you to experiment to suit your own palate.

Fresh cheese and cumin biscuit

My sister Suzi loves cumin in her cheese, especially gouda. These biscuits are flaky pillows that are best eaten still warm, smeared with fresh white cheese and toasted cumin. You can roll, cut and freeze the dough ahead of time and cook them as needed.

YIELD

Makes 16 small biscuits

INGREDIENTS

2 tablespoons cumin seeds (1 for the biscuit base + 1 for seasoning)
70 g (2½ oz) plain (all-purpose) flour
35 g (1¼ oz/⅓ cup) rye flour
½ teaspoon baking powder
pinch of sugar
pinch of sea salt flakes
55 g (2 oz) salted butter, at room temperature and softened, diced
125 g (4½ oz) fresh white cheese (for homemade see page 48), quark or labneh (for homemade see page 67) + 125 g (4½ oz) extra to top the biscuits, at room temperature and softened
2 tablespoons beef fat/tallow (or Copha/vegetable shortening if you'd prefer vegetarian), at room temperature and softened
sea salt flakes

METHOD

In a small frying pan over medium heat, lightly toast the cumin seeds until fragrant. Allow to cool, then crush lightly in a mortar and pestle and set aside

Sift the flours and baking powder together into a bowl and add the sugar and salt.

In a food processor or using electric beaters, cream together the butter, cheese and beef fat until fluffy. Fold the flour through the butter mixture, rubbing it together with your hands. Add 1 tablespoon of the cumin and some salt and stir it through. Wrap and rest the dough in the refrigerator for at least an hour or overnight.

Preheat the oven to 220°C (430°F). Line a baking tray with baking paper.

Roll the dough out between two sheets of greaseproof paper to 5–8 mm (¼–½ in) thick. Cut out circles using a 5–6 cm (2–2½ in) round cutter, or cut into small squares, then lie flat on the baking tray. (Any dough scraps can be rested again, re-rolled and used to cut out more shapes.). Bake for 9–10 minutes until puffy and golden on the base. Transfer to a wire rack to cool.

Smear with the extra fresh white cheese and sprinkle with sea salt flakes and cumin. Serve while still warm.

Keep in an airtight container for up to a week and warm them again to freshen before serving.

Clockwise from left: Ants on a log (page 127); Fresh cheese and cumin biscuit (above); Romeo and Juliet (page 126)

Romeo and Juliet

While working in New York I learned about South American cheese and the rich tapestries of each country's dairying through some of the cooks, who were excited to share their cheese stories and culture. Romeu e Julieta is a beautiful Brazilian combination of cheese and guava paste. Made by layering a fresh, white salty cow's cheese and goiabada guava paste on a stick, looking rather like a liquorice allsort, it is usually served as an appetiser or dessert in Brazil. Being in the Southern Hemisphere, tropical fruit and cheese is a pretty delicious combination of sweet, creamy and tangy.

Loquats are a small, fragrant and juicy tropical fruit that grew everywhere when I was kid, and while I didn't like them then, I have grown to appreciate their flavour and their preserving qualities in jams and pastes.

This recipe uses a younger, softer cheese but, as it is quite delicate and fragile, especially when placed on a skewer, you could use a firmer cheese such as Nectar (Holy Goat) or Mont St Francis (Capriole), both washed-rind semi-hard cheeses. A salty tanginess is what you want to balance the sweetness of the fruit.

YIELD

Serves 4–6

INGREDIENTS

160 g (5½ oz) Loquat paste (page 202) – you can use guava or quince paste if you wish, available at specialty grocers
120 g (3½ oz) semi-hard cheese – L'Etivaz or Comté work well
dried pineapple (see page 198)
skewers
120–150 g (4½–5½ oz) goat's cheese – firm curd, log (for homemade see page 63) or semi-hard
a little grated lemon zest + a few drops of fresh lemon juice
sea salt flakes

METHOD

Cut the paste, semi-hard cheese and pineapple into small cubes or triangles – a nice bite-size so you can fit two of each on a skewer that can be eaten in two to three bites.

Layer the skewers with pineapple at the base, then semi-hard cheese, then loquat paste, then goat's cheese and repeat. The pineapple acts as a good base and the goat's cheese is at the top because it's soft.

Season each skewer with lemon zest and each piece of fruit with a drop or two of lemon juice and sea salt flakes.

Ants on a log

Celery, peanut butter and sultanas (golden raisins) — good luck getting me to eat that when I was a kid. This is a grown-up version with blue cheese and cherries. Use a quality, sweeter, softer blue cheese like Gorgonzola Dolce, Bayley Hazen Blue or Berry's Creek Riverine Blue and, if you don't want to make your own dried cherries, you can buy them, or substitute with sultanas or dried white mulberries.

YIELD

Makes 10 small sticks

INGREDIENTS

celery sticks — the ones in between the large outer sticks and hearts work best, but you can use any as long as they hold the cheese and nuts
sea salt flakes
a few drops of fresh lemon juice + a little grated lemon zest
salted roasted peanuts, chopped in half
dried cherries (see note), sliced into small rounds
freshly ground black pepper

BLUE CHEESE WHIP

150 g (5½ oz) blue cheese, soft and sweet, at room temperature
50 g (1¾ oz) crème fraîche (for homemade see page 56) at room temperature
sea salt flakes
freshly ground black pepper

METHOD

For the blue cheese whip, in a food processor whiz the blue cheese until soft, then add the crème fraîche and blend until smooth and spreadable. Don't overwhip or you may have blue cheese butter. Season with salt and pepper. Transfer to a piping (icing) bag. If it's too soft, refrigerate for an hour or so to firm up so it's pipeable.

Peel the celery with a peeler to remove all the stringy bits — you don't have to do this, but it does make it easier to eat when cutting and biting into the sticks. Cut into long batons around 8–9 cm (3¼–3½ in), then lay flat on a tray. Season with salt, then lemon juice.

Pipe three small dots of the blue cheese whip in each piece of celery. Lay three salted peanut halves in the base and squish them in a bit so they are secure.

Pipe a good amount of the blue cheese over the top to cover the nuts, then layer the dried cherries on top. Finish with pepper and lemon zest.

NOTE

Cherries drained from a whey soda, or tinned pitted cherries dried at 85°C (185°F) for 4 hours, still a little bit chewy. Cherries can also be found in health food stores already dried.

Anchovies and cheese

Most chefs love anchovies. They can add salt, meatiness and umami to food, along with being a tasty bite at the start of a meal. Every chef I've worked for has had a memorable anchovy snack on the menu at some point. As with cheese, the quality of the anchovy is what makes it. Of all the anchovies I have worked with, Angelachu and Don Bocarte are my two standouts. But any quality anchovies work.

Haloumi is a salty cheese to begin with, so if you're using a store-bought variety, soak it in plain water for a day or two to pull out some of the brine and saltiness — adding some lemon peel to the soaking liquid will also help. If you are making the grilled cheese recipe from the book (page 86), use less salt when you brine it.

This is a plate of good things to snack. Eat it with your hands and enjoy with a cold beer or glass of something fizzy.

YIELD

Serves 2–4

INGREDIENTS

- 120–160 g (4½–5½ oz) cheese for grilling — haloumi or similar (or see A grilled cheese on page 86)
- 2 slices of sourdough
- 1 garlic clove, cut in half — keep one half for rubbing the bread and Microplane the other half into oil for brushing the cheese as it cooks. You could also use the oil and garlic from the marinated cheese recipe (page 51)
- extra-virgin olive oil
- grapeseed or other neutral oil
- Espelette pepper (see note)
- 1 small tin quality anchovies
- 1 lemon, cut into wedges or cheeks

METHOD

Take the cheese from the brine, pat it dry thoroughly and let it sit at room temperature for a few minutes.

Over a grill or in a hot cast-iron pan over high heat, toast and char the bread so it is nicely browned on the outside but still a little soft on the inside. Rub with the garlic clove and brush with extra-virgin olive oil. The idea is for the toast to take on some of the garlic flavour but not be too soggy with oil.

While the bread is toasting, heat a non-stick frying pan over high heat and add a good splash of grapeseed oil. You will need enough to almost shallow-fry the cheese, so don't use too large a pan. Gently place the cheese in the pan, making sure it is dry so it doesn't spit and flare in the pan. Grill on all sides, caramelising evenly. If you have a barbecue, finish the cheese on that once it has got a crust from the pan. Brush the cheese with the garlic and oil as it is cooking. Once soft and crisp, transfer to paper towel to drain.

Liberally drizzle the olive oil over the cheese, finish with pepper and serve with the anchovies, lemon and toast.

NOTE

Espelette is a sweet, fruity and mild red pepper variety from Espelette, in the northern Basque region of France. Paprika or dried chilli flakes can be substituted.

Truffled cheese

In the last 10 years, black truffles have exploded in Australia, with all states now growing and producing them in the short winter season. They are an expensive little fungus that packs a punch when used well. In cheese it can be a potent addition to a soft, creamy cheese, like Brillat-Savarin aux truffe and coulommiers truffe, firmer cheeses such as Caciotta al Tartufo and gouda with truffle, and the highly pungent, white truffle–infused Moliterno al Tartufo. Soft blue cheese, like Cremoso al Tartufo also are made with truffles infused. Personally I think truffles are at their best when served warm with a rich sauce to release the aroma and flavour. That said, they work well with soft creamy cheese too.

Truffles and cheese marry well, but so do other interesting and pungent flavours that aren't so exclusive and expensive.

Cheesemakers and mongers split open soft cheese to add the truffles to the cheese paste inside, then close them and seal with cream to finish the maturation process. This allows the cheese time to soak up all that aroma and flavour. Too long and the cheese may be overpowered and overripe; too short and the cheese might not pick up as much flavour. Truffles are grown in soil, and can therefore harbour nasty bacteria like listeria, and need to be treated before adding to milk and cheese. It is best to only purchase them from a reputable source and use them fresh. Like cheese, truffles like a moist environment, so keep them covered with a damp towel; putting them in rice drys them out.

YIELD

Makes 1 small cheese to serve 2–4

INGREDIENTS

1 small or large unripened white mould cheese (for homemade see page 74), about 300 g (10½ oz)
fresh black or white truffle, or other chosen aroma
50–100 g (1¾–3½ oz) crème fraîche (for homemade see page 56) or mascarpone, depending on size of cheese

METHOD

Using a small, unripened white mould cheese, around the 3-week mark of maturing – longer if it is a larger wheel – take a small knife to gently mark a line in the middle of the cheese around the entire circumference. Using a length of sterilised wire or fine fishing line, form a loop around the cheese as if you were tying a ribbon around a box, and tighten in one motion as if you were tying a knot. The cheese should now be separated into two identical-sized discs. Flip them over so the paste is facing up.

You could use a black or white truffle on a fine Microplane now if you wish. I prefer grating the truffle in as I find more of the truffle is exposed and the aromas permeate the smaller cheese better, but you can shave them if you wish.

Some other ideas you could try:

dried pine, chanterelle, porcini, shiitake or wild mushrooms – also a good use of any scraps
quality chocolate
fresh or used and dried coffee grounds
dried citrus peel, such as mandarin skin
dried herbs – dry them yourself – fresh herbs will rot and go mouldy in moist cheese
dried onion and other alliums

In a small bowl, mix the crème fraîche or mascarpone until spreadable but not loose.

With a little palette or cheese knife, spread a thin layer of the cream over the bottom half of the exposed cheese, then dust, grate, shave or sprinkle your truffle or flavouring on top. Fold the lid back on and seal up the cut you made earlier, by plastering it up with the cream. Make sure it is sealed but don't go to overboard with the cream.

Once it is completely sealed, rewrap in cheese paper and continue to slowly age for another 1–2 weeks or until ripe and pungent. Serve at room temperature or bake.

Cervelle de canut, radishes and brioche

Literally meaning 'silk worker's brain', this is a cheese dish that originated in Lyon in the 19th century and is named for the canuts, or silk workers, of the time. Also called claqueret, it is a cheese dip/spread often eaten with bread, radishes or hot baked potatoes and is made with fromage blanc (fresh white cheese), herbs, pepper and oil.

From the time Melbourne cheesemaker Richard Thomas first taught me how to make fromage blanc, he has been in my brain about this dish. Having never been to Lyon to really experience it in all its glory, this is a version that I like to prepare, serve and eat.

You will need to start the brioche 2 days ahead — same with the cheese. However, hot baked potatoes, grilled bread, crackers, potato chips (crisps) or croquettes are all good alternatives to serve with it at the start of a meal.

YIELD

Serves 4

INGREDIENTS

extra-virgin olive oil
sea salt flakes
freshly ground black pepper
washed radishes

BRIOCHE PULL-APART

250 g (9 oz/1⅔ cups) cake or 00 flour
+ extra for dusting
5 g (⅛ oz) sea salt flakes
25 g (1 oz) sugar
45 ml (1½ fl oz) milk
8 g (¼ oz) fresh yeast
125 g (4½ oz) eggs
50 g (1¾ oz) soft butter in small cubes
+ 145 g (5 oz) butter
50 g (1¾ oz) clarified butter, for brushing

CHEESE DIP

1 large French shallot
1 fermented garlic clove — fresh garlic is fine too
1 tablespoon washed and chopped chervil
1 tablespoon washed and chopped French tarragon
1 tablespoon thinly sliced chives
50 g (1¾ oz) crème fraîche (for homemade see page 56)
splash of walnut oil
1 teaspoon chardonnay or tarragon vinegar, or to taste
200 g (7 oz) fresh white cheese (for homemade see page 48) (see note)
freshly ground black pepper
sea salt flakes

METHOD

This recipe will make enough pastry for six small brioches loaves, and it keeps well in the freezer for a month.

To make the brioche pull-apart, add the flour, salt and sugar to the bowl of a stand mixer and mix together with a spoon.

In a small saucepan over low heat, warm the milk to 37°C (98.6°F), then add the yeast and let it activate for 5 minutes. Add to the flour mixture and start the mixer, fitted with the dough hook, incorporating the ingredients for a couple of minutes.

In a small bowl, lightly beat the eggs, then add to the mixer, a little at a time, until a dough is formed. Slowly mix in the 50 g (1¾ oz) soft butter, a small piece at a time, until incorporated and glossy. Set the dough aside to prove for 1 hour in a lightly greased bowl covered with a damp towel.

While the dough is proving, take the 145 g (5 oz) butter and roll it out roughly into a 12 × 18 cm (4¾ × 7 in) rectangle about 5 mm (¼ in) thick. It doesn't need to be perfect.

Deflate the dough slightly with a rolling pin, wrap it in plastic wrap, and put both the dough and butter sheet in the fridge to rest overnight.

The next day, pull the butter sheet out of the fridge and leave for an hour or so to soften. The butter needs to be pliable, but not soft, to meld into the dough.

Flour a work surface liberally, keeping it well dusted as you go since you don't want the dough to tear. Roll the dough away from you into a rectangle about 32 × 40 cm (12½ × 15¾ in) and 1 cm (½ in) thick. Again, this doesn't need to be perfect — it just needs to be big enough so the butter sheet fits in it. Place the butter sheet in the middle of the dough and fold both ends of the dough over the butter, making sure the seams join together. Rolling away from you, roll the dough and butter out again into another rectangle the same size. Rotate the dough 90 degrees and fold one-third of the pastry into the middle, then the other on top, like you're folding a letter.

Rotate 90 degrees and, with the open end of the dough parcel facing you, roll away from yourself again into another rectangle. Do another letter fold, then wrap in plastic wrap and refrigerate for at least an hour.

Take the dough out and, with the open end facing you, roll into another rectangle and do another letter fold. Refrigerate again. Do this three more times.

The next morning, cut the dough into sixths. With each sixth making one loaf, keep what you need out and freeze or refrigerate the rest for use at a later date.

Roll out the dough on a floured bench until about 3 mm (⅛ in) thick and cut into a rectangle about 15 cm (6 in) wide and 8–10 cm (3¼–4 in) long. Starting from the bottom edge, roll the dough up, like a Swiss roll, and lightly brush the top with melted butter to seal, pinching it closed. Refrigerate to firm up for 15 minutes, then slice across into rounds about 1.5–2 cm (½–¾ in) thick.

Lightly grease and flour a stainless-steel, round cookie cutter about 9–10 cm (3½–4 in) in diameter or a large muffin tin. A larger mould/size will also work but may require a longer cooking time.

Lightly roll the dough coins in your hands into little balls, pinching any ends that come apart, and lay them in the mould set on a tray lined with baking paper. Set the dough aside to prove in a warm place, for 1½–2 hours, or until risen and puffy.

Meanwhile, preheat the oven to 210°C (410°F).

Bake the pastry for 12 minutes, then turn the heat down to 200°C (400°F) and continue baking for a further 4–6 minutes. Remove from the oven and transfer, using an egg flip, to a wire rack. Brush liberally with warm clarified butter and season with salt.

To make the cheese dip, peel and dice the shallot finely. Microplane the garlic and chop all the herbs separately.

In a bowl, soften the crème fraîche with the fresh white cheese to break it up, but don't make it too smooth. Add the oil and vinegar and check the seasoning. Fold through the shallot, garlic and herbs, check the seasoning and refrigerate. Let it sit for a couple of hours for the flavours to develop.

Place the dip in a small bowl, with a good slosh of oil and some black pepper. Serve with the radishes and the brioche, either warm or room temperature, on the side.

NOTE

You can use yoghurt or other fresh curd instead of fresh white cheese — if too thick, thin it out with milk.

Lacto-fermented, pickled and fresh vegetables with curd

Sour things and cheese — two of my favourites. Spicy, acidic vegetables with cool, fresh cheese to drag through while eating with your hands is a fun way to eat. Mum and her friends would whip up dips and chip platters for family and friends' gatherings, birthdays and holidays when I was younger, and Nanna would always have sauerkraut and pickles with her food. I think my love of eating fresh cheese and snacking like this most definitely comes from carrot sticks in a clock-like mosaic with some sort of dip in the middle and the wafts of fermented things coming from the table.

This is a dish that relies on good produce, good markets and/or your own garden. The asparagus that came into season the same time as the broad bean leaves popping up, along with chives, sorrel and shiso and other herbs, made for a fun dish to eat during the photography of the book. Use your imagination. Summer might be cucumbers, dill, tomatoes, peaches and lovage; autumn may be persimmons, watercress and mustard greens; and in winter perhaps it's bitter leaves, citrus, dates and kohlrabi. You could also mix and match the spices and condiments as you wish but I do recommend using something fresh and sweet like the fruit to help balance it all as you are eating. Treat it like a Le Grand Aïoli.

When you make the cheese, yoghurt or curd, hang it in a small cheese hoop or basket just after you make it. You don't need to do this, but it does help firm the cheese up evenly. If you'd prefer a softer, more spreadable cheese, you can whip it slightly in a bowl and dollop it on the plate instead.

YIELD

Serves 4–6

INGREDIENTS

- apples, cherries, grapes, pear, cherry tomatoes, fresh stone fruit or whatever is in season
- fresh, raw seasonal vegetables
- any other spice or seasoning you wish — dried mandarin or citrus peel ground into a powder also work well
- 250 g (9 oz) fresh white cheese (for homemade see page 48), cacioricotta (for homemade see page 66), ricotta or labneh (for homemade see page 67)
- Fermented carrots (page 105)
- Fermented kohlrabi (page 105)
- Pickled beetroot (page 108)
- splash of quality olive oil — a delicate green arbequina or something similar
- pinch of dried chilli flakes, Aleppo pepper or Espelette pepper (see note on page 128)
- pinch of cumin seeds, lightly toasted and gently crushed in a mortar and pestle
- pinch of fennel seeds, lightly crushed, or fennel pollen
- leaves and herbs
- a small chunk of honeycomb

METHOD

Cut the fruit and vegetables as you arrange the ingredients on the platter so you can see the shape that works. Drizzle with the oil and add the spices and other ingredients.

Red pepper and cream cheese dip

One of my first kitchen jobs was at an extremely busy bistro inside a pub in Perth, Western Australia. A trio of dips was on the menu, and most tables ordered it, especially those enjoying a long boozy lunch on Fridays. We would make hummus, feta and yoghurt and red pepper dip – bucket-loads of them at a time. The red pepper dip was the dip I dreaded most – a large Robot Coupe stick blender, 5 kg (11 lb) of Philly cream cheese, boxes of roasted red capsicums and bottles of sweet chilli sauce all pushed through a chinois into a 20 litre (5¼ gallon) bucket. To date, this is one of the messiest and least desirable jobs I've ever had to do, and I still despise those blenders.

This version is a little friendlier on the white shirt and is delicious with warm toasted flatbreads, vegetables or, even better, with hot chips (fries).

You will need to start the red capsicums 2–3 days ahead.

YIELD

Serves 2–4 as a small starter

INGREDIENTS

4 large red capsicums (bell peppers)
1 long red chilli
sea salt flakes
splash of whey (optional)
splash of sherry vinegar
1–3 teaspoons sugar
½ teaspoon smoked paprika
100 g (3½ oz) cream cheese (for homemade see page 64), at room temperature so it is smooth and spreadable – thin out with a splash of buttermilk or milk if needed
extra-virgin olive oil
warm grilled bread, to serve

METHOD

Preferably over an open flame, gently blister the skins of the capsicums and long red chilli – being careful not to take them too far – so they are easily peeled but not mush. You can also do this in a hot oven. Once the skin is loose, place in a bowl, cover with plastic wrap and set aside to steam. Once cool, peel them (see note), remove the seeds and core, then chop them in a food processor to a pulp, but don't puree.

Put the mixture in a small saucepan over low heat for a few minutes, stirring with a spatula to draw out some of the moisture so you have more of a paste than a liquid. Spread the mixture out on a flat tray and leave to cool. Once cool, weigh it and add 3% of its weight in salt, a splash of whey (not necessary but it will speed up the ferment) and place in a sterilised jar with a small piece of baking paper on top to help prevent bacterial growth. Cover with a lid and leave to ferment for 2–3 days, opening occasionally to burp, until it has a nice tang and flavour.

Strain the mix through a fine sieve to remove any moisture, then transfer to a blender and process together with the vinegar, sugar, smoked paprika and salt to taste. If you'd like a spicier version, add a little dried chilli. (It should last in the refrigerator for a couple of weeks and can be used in place of mild hot sauce.)

The cream cheese needs to be room temperature to whisk it slightly and soften it. Add 2–4 tablespoons (or more or less) of the capsicum sauce to the cheese and swirl it through lightly. If you want a more incorporated dip, stir vigorously or blend in a food processor. Serve as is in a bowl, drizzled with olive oil and salt with warm grilled bread on the side.

NOTE

If you like, reserve the skins. Burn them fully in a hot oven and then dry out at 85°C (185°F) until completely dry. Blitz in a spice grinder and keep in an airtight container. The powder can be used for rubbing into cheese rinds, seasoning or dusting.

Wagyu bresaola with marinated cheese

Bresaola is air-dried salumi that is often served with a salty, firm cheese like Parmigiano-Reggiano and, when made with quality wagyu or marbled beef it is quite extraordinary. Hot summer nights remind me of plates of brawn (head cheese), salami, ham, kransky and Polish sausage being laid out for dinner with a salad. It's too hot to cook, and sometimes even too hot to eat in Australia in summer.

When I worked on the meat slicer at Cumulus in Melbourne, there was often a slice of wagyu bresaola to taste, as it had oxidised from the previous cut. Made with high-quality girello or eye of round, the beef is cleaned, trimmed, salted and spiced, then hung and air-dried like prosciutto. When sliced into, the marbling and intermuscular fat make it look like the view from above a river system on Mars.

During the bushfires on the east coast of Australia in 2019–2020, there was a bunch of Australian cooks working at Estela and Flora Bar with Ignacio Mattos in New York. We were shocked by what was happening at home and wanted to help in any way we could. Ignacio generously allowed us to use Estela to put on a fundraising dinner. My dear friend Sam Lawrence, the chef de cuisine, and Lachie Cameron, the sous, helped create a wonderful Australian-influenced menu and the team pulled off a very special and fun night. We made some cheese and had another Australian – Ollie from A Smallgood in Maine – make some beautiful bresaola. I can't remember how we served it that night but everything served together with good potato chips (crisps) and a cool lager on a hot summer's night is a good idea, preferably by the beach.

YIELD

Serves 2–4 as a starter

INGREDIENTS

50 g (1¾ oz) Persian feta/marinated cheese (for homemade see page 51) + some of the peppercorns, oil and confit garlic from the jar
100 g (3½ oz) wagyu bresaola (see note)
sea salt flakes
zest of ½ lemon
a few rocket (arugula) or mustard leaves
quality potato chips (crisps) or bread, to serve

METHOD

Dollop the cheese on the base of the plate, breaking it up with some of the oil, herbs, pepper and garlic from the jar.

Take the thinly sliced bresaola and fold, twist and turn it to lay it over and around the cheese.

Dress the rocket leaves with salt, lemon zest and the oil from the cheese jar, then scatter on top of the meat. Serve with potato chips or bread.

NOTE

Slice thinly as close to serving as possible as it will quickly oxidise and discolour.

Old dairy cow tartare with cultured cream and sorrel

Txuleta beef is from mature dairy cattle and is known for its rich and intense flavour, deep colouring and golden fat. Originating in the Basque region of Spain, the tradition is becoming a way of using 'retired' dairy cows in other parts of the world.

Steak tartare is a lean dish and, when combined with the toasty crunch of the buckwheat, the spicy sourness of fermented chilli, the tang and fattiness of cultured cream, and the freshness of the sorrel leaves, this makes for a delicious and fun version.

YIELD

Serves 2–4

INGREDIENTS

120 g (4½ oz) cleaned grass-fed rump or fillet (tenderloin) – you want a cut that is tender and doesn't have much fat or muscle – dry-aged is good; just be sure to trim off all the age (if you can't find retired dairy beef, a good grass-fed and finished Black Angus or even water buffalo is a good substitute)
20 g (¾ oz) table salt
10 g (¼ oz) sugar
6–8 sorrel leaves
iced water
20 g (¾ oz) white onion, diced
sea salt flakes
zest of ½ lemon
1 tablespoon olive oil
a few drops of fish sauce
a few drops of cabernet sauvignon vinegar (Forvm brand if possible)
a small knife tip amount of kanzuri or red yuzu koshu, or to taste (see notes)
8–10 g (¼ oz) soba/buckwheat tea (see notes)
1 egg yolk, whisked – you may not need it all
2 tablespoons cultured cream (for homemade see page 56)
grilled bread (optional)

METHOD

Ask your butcher to clean the beef or do it yourself. Trim off any sinew, fat and dry aged pieces.

Mix the salt and sugar to make a cure, then lightly season the beef all over and place on a rack in the fridge for an hour. (The rack prevents the beef from sitting in the liquid that will be drawn out, and the curing helps season and firm up the texture.) After an hour, brush off the cure, lightly rinse the meat and pat dry. You can do this ahead of time, but no more than 12–24 hours as the beef will discolour.

Wash and soak the sorrel leaves in iced water to freshen them up, then leave them to drip and air-dry on a rack. Don't use a salad spinner as they bruise easily.

Using a sharp knife, chop the beef into small dice about 3–5 mm (⅛–¼ in), then place in a small stainless-steel bowl. Season the beef and onion with a small pinch of salt and lemon zest, mix well, breaking up the beef, then add the olive oil, fish sauce and vinegar. Mix and taste. The add the kanzuri and mix again.

If the seasoning is good, add the soba and mix through and check the seasoning again. Add the egg yolk at the end to add richness but be careful not to mix it too much or it will begin to emulsify and become tacky. The seasoning should be quite sharp but balanced with the fat of the cream. Spoon onto the plate with a good dollop of the cultured cream, and more lemon zest. Serve the sorrel leaves and grilled bread, if desired. Roll the beef in the leaves and eat with your hands.

NOTES

Kanzuri is a traditional fermented chilli condiment that is made with peppers, salt, koji and yuzu, similar to yuzu koshu. Red yuzu koshu is a good substitute if you can't find it in specialty Japanese grocers.

Soba is buckwheat tea made from roasted buckwheat kernels and can be found in Asian grocers.

Fermented farro and walnut salad with carrots, apricot and yoghurt

In kitchens where I worked in New York, we would use beautiful organic, native and freshly stone-milled heirloom grains and legumes from Anson Mills. Farro piccolo is one that I remember the most – an ancient grain that has a sweet, nutty flavour, with a good amount of chew that is fairly easy to prepare.

If you are using unfermented farro, you'll need to soak the grains or cook for a touch longer.

Mix and match the seeds, nuts, herbs and dressings as you wish. Add or subtract anything you like – just make sure the salad is dressed and seasoned well.

YIELD

Makes enough for a large bowl for 4 people

INGREDIENTS

125 g (4½ oz/½ cup) whole organic farro (see notes)
½ tablespoon whey
sea salt flakes
olive oil
100 g (3½ oz) walnuts
45 g (1½ oz) sunflower seeds
300 ml (10 fl oz) cottonseed oil or similar, for frying
50 g (1¾ oz/¼ cup) black rice
120 g (4½ oz) Fermented baby carrots (page 105) – about a bunch (see notes)
½ bunch parsley or 3 tablespoons chopped
½ bunch mint or 3 tablespoons chopped
1 bunch coriander (cilantro)
1 bunch spring onion (scallion) whites only, sliced into rounds
3–4 large kale leaves
zest of 1 orange + orange juice if needed
170–200 ml (6–7 fl oz) Apricot and honey dressing (page [illegible]6)
80–100 g (2¾–3½ oz) labneh yoghurt (for homemade see page 67), yoghurt or Yoghurt cheese (page 69)
dried orange powder or bee pollen

METHOD

Ferment the farro grains for 1–2 days in a glass jar or container with 750 ml (25½ fl oz/3 cups) of water and the whey until they have a lactic smell and fizz, then drain and discard the brine.

In a pot, bring 2 litres (68 fl oz/8 cups) of water to the boil with a pinch of salt and cook the farro until soft, about 35–40 minutes. Drain and spread out on a tray with a drizzle of olive oil and set aside to cool.

Toss the walnuts with some olive oil and salt on a baking tray and bake in a 180°C (350°F) oven for 6–8 minutes until toasted. Allow to cool. Toast the sunflower seeds at the same temperature for the same time and also cool.

Heat the cottonseed oil in a small, deep pan to 210°C (410°F). Carefully drop the rice in and fry for 30 seconds. It will boil up quickly and then subside as the rice puffs, for about 5–10 seconds, until all the grains have puffed. Pour the oil and rice through a mesh strainer into another pot that is large enough to hold the hot oil, then drain the rice on paper towel.

Slice the carrots into rounds, chop the herbs, spring onion and kale, and roughly chop the walnuts.

In a large bowl, mix the grains, puffed rice, walnuts and seeds with the carrots. Season with sea salt flakes and the zest of the orange and mix well to combine. Add the herbs and dress with the apricot dressing to coat thoroughly. Check the seasoning – the acidity should be enough but add a squeeze of orange juice if you'd like. Serve in a bowl with yoghurt, sprinkled with dried orange or bee pollen on top and drizzled with olive oil.

NOTES

Farro can also be cooked from raw or lightly soaked. Other whole grains, such as barley, can also be substituted but cooking time and flavour may vary.

Just-cooked, roasted or pickled carrots can be substituted.

Cacioricotta with tomatoes, anchovies and green sauce

When tomatoes and herbs are at their peak, there is not much you need to do, except make a little cheese. You can omit the anchovies and capers if you wish, but I'd advise you not to.

Make sure you use the best of everything here — the tomatoes need to be bursting with flavour, the anchovies plump, the herbs and green sauce vibrant and delicious — and splash with a quality olive oil to round it out (something fresh, peppery and robust).

YIELD

Serves 4—6

INGREDIENTS

½ garlic clove
sea salt flakes
10—15 capers, soaked and drained if salted
1 bunch flat-leaf (Italian) parsley, picked and washed
½ bunch mint, picked and washed
1 bunch basil
2½ tablespoons cabernet sauvignon vinegar (Forvm brand if possible)
extra-virgin olive oil, plus 50—75 ml (1¾—2½ fl oz), to dress
zest and juice of ½ lemon
freshly ground black pepper
600 g (1 lb 5 oz) ripe heirloom tomatoes (about 5—6)
200—250 g (7—9 oz) cacioricotta (for homemade see page 66), at room temperature (store-bought buffalo ricotta is a good substitute)
4 quality anchovy fillets
chilli flakes, to sprinkle (optional)

METHOD

In a mortar and pestle, smash the garlic with a pinch of salt, then add the capers and grind to a rough paste.

Lightly chop the parsley before transferring to the mortar and pestle, in stages, and smash with the pestle before preparing the mint and basil in the same way.

Add some of the vinegar and olive oil as you go, then add the rest once you have a green sauce with a nice pesto-like consistency. Add the lemon zest and juice.

Check the final seasoning, as it may need more salt, vinegar or oil, and finish with a good amount of freshly ground black pepper.

Slice and core the tomatoes and lay them out on a tray and season each piece with salt. Lay the tomatoes out on a platter and dollop or spread the cacioricotta cheese over them, then dress everything with the green sauce and a splash of vinegar and more olive oil.

Cut the anchovies in half lengthways, or thirds if they are large, and drape them over the cheese. Finish with more pepper and chilli flakes if you wish.

Burrata curd with peas, broad beans and bottarga

The combination of fish and cheese is quite a topic — some say never, others say occasionally, and with some classic dishes combining the two, such as moules au Roquefort, lobster mornay, anchovies with mozzarella, or even smoked salmon and cream cheese, I agree.

The cheese and seafood should complement each other and, when done well, cheese and seafood works, especially when it comes to creamy curds and dried, salty fish.

Good fresh peas at the start of spring are so sweet and crunchy straight from the pod, and can be eaten like candy. I love the texture and it reminds me of lunches at Nanna's house, along with shelled broad beans from her garden. Just be careful how many beans you eat in a sitting; my brother Mick has a funny story about that.

Bottarga is dried mullet roe, mojama is cured tuna loin, which also works well, and, failing that, fresh, cured trout roe is also delicious in its place.

YIELD

Serves 2–4 as a side

INGREDIENTS

60 g (2 oz) fresh peas (see notes)
60 g (2 oz) broad beans
sea salt flakes
zest and juice of 1 lemon
2 teaspoons Mint vinegar (page 108) or chardonnay vinegar (Forvm brand if possible)
100–120 g (3½–4½ oz) Quick mozzarella (page 85), stracciatella, or a burrata ball broken open and torn
a few baby mint leaves
pea shoots/broad bean leaves/pea flowers
bottarga (see notes)

SPRING ONION OIL

bunch of spring onions (scallions)
grapeseed oil

METHOD

To make the spring onion oil, weigh the green tops of the spring onions, then weigh twice that amount of grapeseed oil, so a 2:1 ration. Warm the oil in a saucepan to 60°C (140°F), then pour over the greens in a blender. Carefully blend the oil for 2 minutes, then strain through a coffee filter. Put the strained mixture in the freezer for the liquids to freeze, then strain off the oil again. As you only need 2 tablespoons, the rest keeps best in the freezer.

Peel and pod the peas and broad beans, being careful not to eat too many peas while doing so.

Blanch the larger peas in boiling salted water for 10 seconds and refresh in iced water. Any smaller ones you can keep raw, and do the same with the broad beans — but cook longer until just cooked. If the broad beans are quite large and the skin is thick, pod them again once refreshed.

In a small bowl, toss the peas and broad beans with salt and half the lemon zest, then add a squeeze of lemon juice, the vinegar and 2 tablespoons of the spring onion oil and let marinate for a couple of minutes — make it sharp, as the bottarga is salty and the fat comes from the rich cheese.

Spoon the cheese into a bowl, then the salad over the top with a few of the mint leaves and pea shoots.

Using a Microplane, zest more lemon and then sprinkle the bottarga quite liberally over the top just as you are ready to serve.

NOTES

If you can't find good fresh peas, a quickly blanched frozen pea will also work — they just have a different texture and flavour.

Bottarga can found at certain fishmongers and specialty stores and lasts in the fridge. It's also great with ricotta or left-over burrata curds on toast.

Burrata curd toast with watermelon rind mostarda and capers

Stephanie Alexander is one of Australia's most well-known and loved cooks. Coincidentally, she also co-ran Richmond Hill Cafe and Larder, which housed Melbourne's first cheese room. Her *Cook's Companion* was one of the first books I received and started cooking with. In it is a beautiful recipe for pickled watermelon rind that uses the green and white skin that is usually thrown away after a summer barbecue. I love watermelon for breakfast and always have plenty of rind, so this mostarda-style recipe based on Stephanie's is a good way to use it up.

Before leaving New York, the team at Altro Paradiso had a burrata dish with mostarda di Cremona on the menu, where this snack also takes inspiration from. The watermelon mostarda is delicious with pasta filata–style cheese, charcuterie and boiled meats and keeps for months in the refrigerator.

You will need to make the watermelon rind 2 weeks ahead of time.

YIELD

Makes 4 toasts

INGREDIENTS

2 slices sourdough
1 garlic clove, confited or raw
olive oil
250 g (9 oz) Quick mozzarella (page 85), stracciatella, or a burrata ball broken open and torn
12 wild capers in brine — depending on size (see notes)

WATERMELON RIND PICKLE

50 g (1¾ oz) sea salt flakes
500 ml (17 fl oz/2 cups) water
500 g (1 lb 2 oz) watermelon rind, with a little of the pink flesh still on

PICKLING SYRUP

500 g (1 lb 2 oz) raw (demerara) sugar
300 ml (10 fl oz) cider vinegar
300 ml (10 fl oz) water
1 cm (½ in) piece of ginger thinly sliced, and julienned
1½ teaspoons mustard powder
1 teaspoon yellow mustard seeds

METHOD

For the watermelon rind pickle, make a 10% brine with the salt and water, then cut the rind into strips of about 4 × 1 cm (1½ × ½ in). Soak the watermelon rind in the brine overnight in the refrigerator.

The next day, drain the rind, put in a saucepan, cover with cold water and simmer for about 30–40 minutes until the skin is easily pierced all the way through but still holding its shape.

Meanwhile make the pickling syrup by putting all the ingredients in a saucepan, bringing to a simmer and cooking for 10 minutes. Add the drained watermelon rind and slow-boil until completely translucent – about 30 minutes.

Pour into a sterilised jar and cover with liquid. Once cooled, strain out the rind and boil the syrup down for another 20–30 minutes until syrupy and pour back over to cool, before refrigerating.

It needs at least 2 weeks to mature and develop flavour.

On a grill or in a hot chargrill pan over medium heat, give the bread a good crust and char. Cut the garlic clove in half and rub or smear it onto one side of each toast and brush with olive oil. Cut the toasts in half and trim the ends if they are a bit too crunchy. Divide and spoon the cheese evenly between each toast – if it's falling over the sides a little, this is okay.

Dice the mostarda into small pieces and scatter over the cheese, adding a small drizzle of the syrup and mustard seeds too. Dot the cheese with 3 capers (depending on size) per toast and finish with olive oil, a pinch of sea salt flakes and some freshly ground black pepper.

NOTES

Wild capers in brine are available online, if using salted ones, rinse and soak them for a few hours first.

Burrata curd toast with watermelon rind mostarda and capers (page 148)

Grilled cheese and melon (page 152)

Grilled cheese and melon

I know there is already a recipe for grilled cheese in this book (see page 86), but eating cheese on a hot summer's day straight from the barbecue is my idea of a good time. After my pandemic lockdown cheese adventure in 2021, I made and cooked some cheese for my wife Andrea's family at Christmas. It was a very special moment for me to see people I love experiencing something that gave me so much joy during that difficult time. I'll never forget the faces, smiles and feelings that simple grilled cheese gave us all that day.

Christmas is hot in Australia, and the watermelons are so juicy and sweet. Together with the smoky, garlicky, cheese and chilli, it's a delicious combination. In Cyprus, this style of cheese is enjoyed uncooked with melons in salads as it can be crumbled like feta.

There is no complete recipe for this one. It's more like a platter of good things to slurp, tear, swipe and enjoy. You might want a napkin.

If possible, make the honey curd a day ahead as it takes on more flavour and texture with a rest, but the dish is also delicious without it.

YIELD

Serves 2–4

INGREDIENTS

½ red onion, sliced into rings about 3 mm (½ in) thick
iced water
ripe melons — watermelon, rockmelon (cantaloupe), orange candy melon, or other melon of choice
120-180 g (4½–6½ oz) A grilled cheese (page 86) or a quality store-bought haloumi
¼ bunch mint
lime or lemon zest
pinch of dried smoked chilli
50 ml (1¾ fl oz) grapeseed oil
1 garlic clove, grated
1-2 tablespoons Chilli vinegar — see recipe on page 108 (or use the juice from a store-bought jar of pickled chillies)
extra-virgin olive oil

NUT AND HONEY CURD

50 g (1¾ oz) fresh white cheese (for homemade see page 48) — drained to thick labneh consistency
3 g (⅛ oz) honey, or to taste
10 g (¼ oz) almond butter, smooth
salt
lemon juice

METHOD

For the nut and honey curd, in a blender, process the fresh white cheese with the honey and almond butter until smooth. Alternatively, you can use a whisk and small bowl. Season with salt and lemon juice.

Soak the onion rings in iced water for 15 minutes, then drain — this helps reduce some of their pungency and softens them.

Cut the melons into small bite-sized wedges or triangles. You can take the rind off and pickle it if you wish (see page 148). When cutting the melon, get creative — peel a little, cut slices into the peel, stuff the mint into the cuts etc. Season the melon with a pinch of salt, lemon or lime zest and smoked chilli.

Heat a non-stick frying pan over high heat and add a good splash of grapeseed oil. You will need enough to almost shallow-fry the cheese, so don't use too large a pan. Gently place the cheese in the pan, making sure it is dry so it doesn't spit and flare in the pan. Grill on all sides, caramelising evenly. If you have a grill, finish the cheese on that once it has got a crust from the pan. Brush the cheese with the garlic and oil as it is cooking. Once soft and crisp, transfer to paper towel to drain.

Dollop the honey cheese curd on the plate and arrange the melons around with the onion rings. Place the warm cheese on and drizzle everything with the Chilli vinegar and extra-virgin olive, finishing with more dried smoked chilli and mint.

Tear, and swipe through the oil and pickle vinegar like a piece of bread.

Charred brassicas, leaves and tops with salted ricotta

A simple side dish, with tops, greens, smoke and salty cheese. This is best done on a grill but can also be cooked on a gas cooktop sitting on a cake rack — just be sure to have the extraction fan on high. Grilled zucchini (courgette) is a good summer substitute, as is asparagus in spring.

Again, there is no concise recipe for this one, it's basically grilling a bunch of vegetable tops and leaves and dressing them well, before covering them in cheese. Use palate and intuition to prepare them to your liking.

INGREDIENTS

turnip leaves
puntarelle
endive (chicory)
radicchio
kale
mustard greens
cime di rapa
grapeseed oil
sea salt flakes
lemon zest
green arbequina olive oil
cabernet sauvignon vinegar (Forvm brand if possible)
salted ricotta (for homemade see page 103; see note)
freshly ground black pepper
dried chilli
honey, if needed

METHOD

Pick, wash and slightly dry the leaves, then lightly rub or spray with grapeseed oil.

Lay the greens out flat on a wire rack and season with salt. Over a hot grill, or gas burner on high, grill the leaves briefly to give a nice char and even cook. Be careful not to burn them or set them on fire.

Place them into a stainless-steel bowl and, if they are too large, chop them before adding the salt, lemon zest, oil and vinegar. Give the leaves a good massage to allow the dressing to penetrate. More vinaigrette is better than less, to allow them to marinate a bit and soak up with the cheese once they are plated. If you are using really bitter greens, a teaspoon of honey will help round everything out when you are dressing them, but warm it gently first so it coats the greens with the dressing rather than sticking.

Place on a bowl or platter, pour over the vinaigrette and grate the cheese on a fine box grater over the top. Finish with more lemon zest, black pepper and dried chilli.

NOTE

If not making your own, salted ricotta can be bought from specialty delicatessens.

Mac, whey and cheese

If you are beginning to make cheese, you will have times where things don't quite go to plan. Too dry, too soft, cracked, under- or overmatured, aged too quickly and a rind that off are all common in learning about affinage. Cheesemaking isn't just following a recipe, there are many things that can go wrong and inevitably will, at least once or twice. Luckily making mac and cheese is a bit simpler. Fresh black truffles, dried porcini or other wild mushrooms shaved over the top are all very delicious additions.

YIELD
Makes a large bowl for 4 to share

INGREDIENTS
sea salt flakes
100 ml (3½ fl oz) pouring (single/light) cream
300 ml (10 fl oz) whey – or 150 ml (5 fl oz) water + 150 ml (5 fl oz) milk
150 g (5½ oz) (a small wheel) white mould cheese (for homemade see page 74)
40 g (1½ oz) freshly grated Parmigiano-Reggiano + extra to finish – or your own semi-hard cheese (see page 97)
400 g (14 oz) fresh or 200 g (7 oz) dried macaroni
freshly ground black pepper

METHOD
Bring a large pot of water to the boil with a good pinch of salt.

Warm the cream and whey gently together. Break up the white mould cheese and drop it in. Simmer for 2 minutes, then turn off to steep and melt for 10 minutes.

Process in a jug blender or using a stick blender, then strain. (If the cheese you are using has a dried-out rind, this may not fully melt and isn't pleasant in the sauce.)

Pour the sauce back into a saucepan over low heat, add the Parmigiano-Reggiano and gently reduce until it starts to thicken.

While it is reducing, cook the macaroni and strain into the sauce, reserving a little of the pasta water.

Toss the pasta through the sauce, season and add the pasta water to loosen as needed.

Finish with more cheese and some pepper.

Pinto beans with parmesan broth

Baked beans were a staple when I was growing up — a source of carbohydrates before a big gymnastics competition to keep the energy levels up. Later, living in the US opened my eyes to quality dried beans. Some of the most memorable meals cooked by the team at Flora Bar in New York would have to be the black, pinto, gigante bean and egg dishes that were served in the mornings.

When sourcing the beans, look for them in organic grocers, smaller batches and self-serve bins — even when they are dried, the older ones are not as good.

You can also use the beans cooked like this as the base for a soup or stew — just increase the whey/water and add vegetables, ham hock or whatever you like.

You will need to start 1–2 days ahead.

YIELD

Makes a large bowl for 4 to share as a side

INGREDIENTS

200 g (7 oz/1 cup) dried pinto beans (or any other dried bean of your choice)
750 ml (25½ fl oz/3 cups) filtered water
1 tablespoon whey
50 g (1¾ oz) Parmigiano-Reggiano (with some rind) + extra for finishing (ask your cheesemonger for rinds if possible — a good piece in the braise is a nice addition)
2 bay leaves
1 large clove fermented garlic, cut in half or 2 fresh cloves crushed with the back of a knife (skin on is fine)
250–300 ml (8½–10 fl oz/1 cup) parmesan stock or whey 80 g (2¾ oz) butter
1 tablespoon fermented garlic brine (see page 105)
zest of ¼–½ lemon
extra-virgin olive oil
parsley

METHOD

In a large jar or similar, soak the beans in the water with the whey for 24 hours. It may seem like a lot of liquid, but the beans will double in size. Once they have soaked, drain them and rinse lightly.

Trim the rinds off the cheese and set the cheese aside. In a wide-bottomed pot, place the beans, 1 litre (34 fl oz/4 cups) fresh water, the cheese rinds, bay leaves and garlic. You want the beans to be even and well spread across the bottom so they cook evenly. Bring to a gentle boil and then simmer, stirring every so often, until just cooked, around 25–45 minutes, but check them often. As the beans have been fermented, they should take less time than a normal dried bean. Once cooked, turn off the heat, allow to cool in the liquor. (The beans are better the next day as the flavour develops, but can be eaten straight away if you wish.)

When ready, strain the beans, keeping the rinds, bay leaves and garlic with them.

Warm the stock or whey in a saucepan and bring to the boil, then lower to a simmer, whisk the butter in, add the garlic brine, then add the beans, garlic, rinds and bay leaves and warm through, reducing the sauce until rich and coating the beans.

The beans should be cooked and warmed through while still holding their shape, and the sauce should be rich, garlicky and leave you wanting another spoonful.

Season and serve with more cheese, lemon zest, olive oil and parsley.

Clams with green cheese and ham

Sardinia is an island in Italy well known for its famous grass-fed sheep's milk cheese and, a favourite of mine, pecorino. The pairing of this cheese with a rich broth with steamed clams and bread to mop up, is another favourite cheese and seafood combination.

Australia doesn't have the range and sizes of clams that are quite readily available in the colder waters of North America and Europe, so surf clams, vongole and pipis can all be used for this dish in Australia. They will all require purging to remove the grit and sand, which can be done by soaking them in lightly salted cool water for a few hours or overnight. Ask your fishmonger first, as this may have already been done for you.

Clams cook quickly, so you want to have everything ready to go for cooking and serving so you don't overcook them, or they go cold. Use a wide-based pot so it doesn't lose too much heat when the clams are added, and they steam open evenly. The clams and sauce will cool quickly, so warm your serving bowl as you are cooking them.

Serve with a glass of funky, skin-contact Vermintino and a bowl for the shells.

YIELD

Serves 2–4

INGREDIENTS

1 bunch English spinach, stems left on, washed
1 bunch tarragon or chervil, picked and washed
100 ml (3½ fl oz) whey
20 g (¾ oz) lardo, cut into 5 mm (¼ in) dice (see notes)
2 tablespoons neutral oil, such as grapeseed
70 g (2½ oz) thick mayonnaise, at room temperature (for homemade see page 117)
15 g (¼ oz) fresh, finely grated Pecorino Sardo (see notes)
500 g (1 lb 2 oz) clams, vongole or pipis, purged
a good splash (50 ml/1¾ fl oz) Pernod or white wine
juice of ½ lemon
1–2 tablespoons garlic brine, liquid or juice (see page 105)
fish sauce, to taste
crusty baguette, to mop up the sauce

METHOD

In a blender on high, process the raw spinach, herbs and whey for 1 minute, then pass through a fine-mesh strainer to make a green whey. This can be done ahead of time and even frozen. (Any left over can be blended with more whey, yoghurt and a banana for a green breakfast smoothie.)

Keep the green whey out at room temperature because cold whey will cool the sauce down too much and heating it too much may cause it to brown.

In a heavy wide-based saucepan with a lid over low heat, gently render the lardo in the oil until translucent.

In a large stainless-steel bowl, whisk together the mayonnaise and finely grated pecorino. Have a fine-mesh strainer ready.

Once the lardo is clear, turn the heat up to high and, when hot, gently place the clams in so you don't smash the shells. Put a lid on and steam over high heat for 60–90 seconds until the clams have all opened.

Carefully strain the liquid into a jug, put the clams gently back in the pan and return to the stove with no heat. Put the stainless-steel bowl with the mayonnaise over the top, keeping the clams warm while also warming the mayonnaise. Slowly add the hot stock and green whey, whisking until you have a thick, foamy green sauce. Season with lemon juice, Pernod, garlic brine and fish sauce.

Add the clams to the sauce, toss together and place in a warmed bowl. Spoon any remaining sauce over each clam. Serve with a crusty baguette and a bowl for the shells.

NOTES

Lardo is cured pork back fat, and can be found at specialty butcher shops.

Grana Padano can be substituted for Pecorino Sardo.

Cheese dumplings and nettles

Gnudi, malfatti or dumplings? For me, it's the silky ricotta dumplings at Estela or the rich malfatti at Altro in New York. Gnudi are made by burying ricotta under semolina so the cheese absorbs the semolina, giving them a heavier bite. The recipe for these dumplings comes from a mixture of the two varieties from Ignacio Mattos's kitchens in New York.

If you make the grilled cheese recipe on page 86, you will end up with whey that can be heated to 92–93°C (198–199°F) and coagulated in 40 ml (1¼ fl oz) vinegar in 80 ml (2½ fl oz/⅓ cup) water to obtain the last remaining curds. Let it sit for 10 minutes, then scoop off the curds and place them in a ricotta basket to drain and refrigerate overnight. If you don't have grilled-cheese whey, you can use a store-bought whey ricotta for this recipe.

Nettles are usually found in springtime on dairy farms and sometimes in the market. There are fine hairs on the leaves and stems that sting, so use gloves when handling them. Amaranth, silverbeet (Swiss chard) or spinach can be substituted.

YIELD

Makes 20 dumplings (see notes)

INGREDIENTS

250 g (9 oz) whey cheese or ricotta – the grilled cheese recipe on page 86 with 4 litres (135 fl oz) milk will yield 250 g (9 oz)
1 egg yolk
50 g (1¾ oz) finely grated hard cheese, such as Grana Padano
25 g (1 oz) 00 flour + extra for rolling
nasturtium leaves, sorrel, wood sorrel or other weeds
grated Parmigiano-Reggiano
grated lemon zest
freshly ground black pepper

NETTLE SAUCE

150 g (5½) picked stinging nettles
iced water
400 ml (13½ fl oz) whey
60 g (2 oz) butter
garlic brine (see page 105)

METHOD

You will need to start these 3 days ahead – a day extra if you make the cheese.

For the dumplings, take your cheese or ricotta from the basket and place in cheesecloth to drain. Bundle it up into a ball and give it a good squeeze to begin to pull out some of the moisture. Place in a colander or on a draining tray and press with a heavy weight – a full jar or tin works well. Press overnight, then unwrap the next day to 'fluff' up the cheese before rewrapping and pressing again, and then again on the second day.

On the third day, in a large bowl or stand mixer, whip the cheese to break it up and soften. Add the egg and beat for another couple of minutes until smooth. Mix the grated cheese and flour together in a separate bowl with a pinch of salt, then add to the dough mix and mix on slow for a further 3 minutes. Wrap the dough and refrigerate for 30 minutes. The dough will be quite moist, so with floured hands and benchtop, roll the dough into small balls of about 15 g (½ oz) each and place them on a lightly floured tray in the freezer. Once frozen, pack them in containers so they don't get freezer burn. They should last for a couple of weeks.

For the nettle sauce, carefully pick and wash the nettles and blanch them in a pot of boiling salted water for a minute. Refresh in iced water and squeeze out most of the moisture. Reduce the whey by half in a saucepan over medium heat, then add the nettles and cook for 1 minute. Being careful because of the steam and heat, combine the mixture in a blender until smooth, then strain to use straight away or chill over an ice bath for later use.

While the sauce is warm, whisk in the butter and garlic brine and season. Bring a large pot of salted water to a light boil. Cook the dumplings for 3–3½ minutes until they float to the surface, then very gently place them in the nettle sauce using a slotted spoon.

Gently place them in a warm bowl with the sauce, leaves, grated cheese, lemon zest and pepper and serve.

NOTES

If doubling the dumpling recipe, which I often do, use a whole egg, and keep the other half of the dough for tomato sauce or your favourite pasta sauce.

It seems like a long time, but if you shorten the dumplings will have more bite and a thicker skin like gnudi due to higher moisture

Shakshuka – baked eggs with tomato, capsicums and yoghurt cheese

Shakshuka is a dish that originates from Tunisia and Northern Africa and is very popular for a hearty breakfast, brunch and lunch in the Middle East and the world over. Usually cooked and served in a pan, the just-set eggs, rich spicy tomato and yoghurt is best served with warm bread for dipping and mopping up the rich sauce.

Having cooked many versions on menus – some with no harissa, some with saffron, some without, and some with no capsicums, this is the version I like to cook and eat. Some recipes call for fresh tomatoes, others tinned tomatoes, but you can use either.

YIELD

Makes 2 pans – enough for 4 to share

INGREDIENTS

2 tablespoons cumin seeds
1 brown onion
2 garlic cloves
50 ml (1¾ fl oz) extra-virgin olive oil
sea salt flakes
2 red capsicums (bell peppers), deseeded and cut into 2 cm (¾ in) dice
1 tablespoon Le Phare du Cap Bon Harissa paste (see note)
2 × 400 g (14 oz) tins whole tomatoes or 800 g (1 lb 12 oz) fresh, ripe tomatoes
freshly ground black pepper
chilli powder (optional)
6 eggs, at room temperature
labneh (for homemade see page 67), yoghurt or Yoghurt cheese (page 69)
½ bunch coriander (cilantro), washed and chopped
1 tablespoon smoked paprika
toasted bread, to serve

METHOD

Toast the cumin seeds in a small pan until fragrant, then transfer to a mortar and pestle and lightly crush them. Cut the onion in half and slice thinly using a mandoline or sharp knife. Do the same with the garlic cloves.

In a heavy, wide-based pan or pot, warm the olive oil, then add the onion with a pinch of salt and slowly cook until translucent. Add the garlic and do the same. Turn the heat up to medium and add the capsicum to fry until soft. Add the crushed cumin, fry for a minute, then add the harissa paste and cook for a further minute, until aromatic.

Pour in the tomatoes and cook them down, stirring often and scraping the sides of the pan with a rubber spatula to prevent burning and catching. Season with salt and pepper and taste and adjust after 15–20 minutes of cooking. If you like it spicier, add a pinch of chilli. You can either cool the sauce down and use later or cook the dish straight away.

Preheat the oven to 220°C (430°F).

In a cast-iron frying pan, ceramic or terracotta pan, warm half the sauce over medium heat so it is hot then, using the back of a spoon, make three divots in the sauce and crack the eggs in. If the eggs are too cold, they won't cook evenly, and the yolk will overcook – even more so if the sauce has been cooled first – so heat it back up if you made it in advance. Repeat in a second pan if making two.

Place the pan in the oven for 10–12 minutes until the whites are cooked and the yolks are still runny.

Spoon on the labneh or break up the yoghurt cheese and scatter it over the pan, along with the chopped coriander, then finish with sea salt, pepper, a dust of paprika and a drizzle of the cheese oil. Serve with warm toasted bread.

NOTE

Harissa paste is a spicy chilli paste from Tunisia that can be found in grocers, or you can make your own.

Steak with pepper sauce and cheese rinds

'Always taste the rind, that's where the labour is.' — Mateo Kehler, Jasper Hill Farm

My first taste of this rather serious combination was with Jake Nemmers at Flora Bar in New York — wagyu flap steak with Taleggio and a beautiful dried tomato, and then another steak dish with a custard condiment that was made from all the Bayley Hazen blue cheese rinds trimmed off for the endive salad.

For me cooking and enjoying steak up to this point was more with French and British condiments — béarnaise, mustard, Café de Paris butter, pepper sauce and the good old tomato sauce bottle at the barbecue. Maybe the familiarity of flavour in this dish comes from beef stroganoff and my grandmother's cooking, but more likely it comes from my love of a good cheeseburger. Wherever it comes from, I've loved the combination of funky cheese and beef ever since.

Taleggio and washed-rind can sometimes have a really sharp, salty, crystallised, dark and funky rind that is unpleasant and bitter, so the rind is usually cut off. The Sergio Arrigoni Taleggio cheese that we would get from our supplier Chris Killoran at Chef Collective was nothing like that. It was so soft, delicate and creamy that it seemed a shame to trim so much off.

We started to use the whole cheese with the rind in the sauces and the results were still silky, funky and delicious. Then with the wild blue cheese rinds too. Washed-rind cheese can be punchy and sometimes bright orange, so a blend of rinds might be needed to balance it out and any left-over custard can be used as a dip, sauce or even served with a pastry.

The pepper sauce takes the lead from an old Cutler & Co recipe that has seen many iterations in Andrew McConnell's restaurants across Melbourne. It needs some love and attention in preparation — low and slow, take your time and don't rush it. The steak, however, needs fast, high heat to get a nice crust and then it needs a good rest. A charcoal grill is a good idea but not essential.

Make the cheese sauce a day ahead or in the morning, so it has time to set.

YIELD

The cheese custard and pepper sauce serve 4–6. The pepper sauce can be frozen, and you can use left-over cheese custard as a dip, especially with hot chips (fries).

INGREDIENTS

ribeye, sirloin or hanger steak work well but any size or cut suitable for grilling will work — it is quite rich with the pepper and cheese, so bear that in mind when choosing the breed, size, marbling and cut
olive oil
sea salt flakes

PEPPER SAUCE

75 g (2¾ oz) garlic, finely diced
110 g (4 oz) French shallots, finely diced
90 g (3 oz) butter
50 ml (1¾ fl oz) grapeseed oil
40 g (1½ oz) sugar
30 ml (1 fl oz) whisky
250 ml (8½ fl oz/1 cup) brown chicken stock
8 g (¼ oz) white peppercorns, gently cracked in a mortar and pestle
8 g (¼ oz) black peppercorns, gently cracked in a mortar and pestle
a pinch of dried used coffee grounds
100 ml (3½ fl oz) white soy sauce
40 ml (1½ fl oz) cabernet sauvignon vinegar (Forvm brand if possible)
pinch of Espelette pepper (see note on page 128) or dried chilli
fish sauce

CHEESE CUSTARD

125 g (4½ oz) washed-rind cheese (for homemade see page 93) — don't use any that are overripe and ammoniated, or with rind that is too funky or wildly orange (unless of course, that is your thing), as this can be quite overpowering if using dry-aged beef; something milder would be more suitable

4 egg yolks

125 ml (4 fl oz) pouring (single/light) cream

METHOD

For the pepper sauce, gently sweat off the garlic and shallots in the butter and oil in a pan over medium–low heat until translucent. Add the sugar and whisky and deglaze the pan for a minute. Add the chicken stock and reduce the liquid down slowly to one-third of its volume. Add the cracked peppercorns, coffee grounds and season with the white soy sauce and the vinegar. The sauce is best made the day before, so it has time to develop flavour.

For the cheese custard, leave the cheese out unwrapped to temper for 30 minutes, then break it apart with clean hands.

Over a water bath, whisk the yolks and cream to bring them together, then switch to a spatula or wooden spoon to stir and gently cook the custard to 78°C (172°F). Take off the heat and break the cheese up further in the sauce to steep for a minute. Place in a blender and process on the lowest setting to bring together. Season and strain, then put a sheet of baking paper directly on top to prevent a skin forming. If you cook it at a high temperature, it can scramble and become grainy, so best to do it gently.

On the day, temper the steak on a rack for 45 minutes to bring it up to room temperature. This helps in achieving a good sear, and allows for even cooking as the steak is relaxed and an even temperature. When ready, brush with oil and plenty of sea salt flakes on both sides. Bring the cheese custard to slowly temper to room temperature at the same time, and constantly stir it to allow it to loosen and temper evenly. Do not leave it near the grill or stove though, as it will melt in parts and you want it to do that on the steak.

On a hot grill or in a chargrill pan over high heat, sear and build a nice crust on both sides of the steak and cook until medium–rare (55–60°C/131–140°F) or your preferred degree of doneness. Rest the steak on a rack for 10 minutes to avoid steaming and overcooking.

Warm the pepper sauce gently and make sure the cheese custard isn't cold. Don't heat it though or the sauce may separate.

Reheat the steak on the grill, in the pan or in a hot oven. You just want to put the heat back into it, not continue cooking.

Carve the steak, pat it dry and season with sea salt flakes. Place the carved steak on a warm plate with a good dollop of cheese custard and a few spoons of pepper sauce. Finish with a drizzle of olive oil and serve.

Fig leaf cheese

Fig leaf has such a beautifully unique flavour and aroma. Fig leaf sap is a coagulant, so if you add it to cold milk it will curdle the milk. Delicious in ice cream, the fig leaf needs be heated in the milk for the flavour to infuse. I think it works beautifully with cheese too.

This can also be made with dried apricot, plum, loquat and other aromatic leaves if you have access to them — wash and dry them in a dehydrator or low oven first.

YIELD

Makes 4–8 small cheeses depending on the basket size, about 250 g (9 oz)

INGREDIENTS

- 1 litre (34 fl oz/4 cups) milk
- 100 g (3½ oz) fig leaves, washed thoroughly in iced water, then air dried
- 100 g (3½ oz) fig leaves (25 g/1 oz for the cheese + 25 g/1 oz for the dried leaves + 50 g/1¾ oz for the oil)
- 200 ml (7 fl oz) grapeseed oil
- iced water
- 2–3 very ripe, jammy black figs (see note)
- vincotto or aged balsamic vinegar
- olive oil
- sea salt flakes
- freshly ground black pepper
- grilled bread, to serve
- honey (optional)

METHOD

Following the fresh white cheese recipe (page 48), bring the milk up to 85°C (185°F), then drop 25 g (1 oz) of the fig leaves in. Cover the pot with a lid, remove from the heat and set aside for 30 minutes to allow the milk to infuse with the leaves. Cool to 25°C (77°F), then strain out the leaves before continuing with the fresh white cheese recipe.

Take another 25 g (1 oz) of fig leaves and dry on racks in an 85°C (185°F) oven for 30 minutes to an hour until completely dry but still green. You can also do this in a microwave. Once dry, blitz them in a blender into a powder.

Warm the grapeseed oil in a small saucepan over low heat to 60°C (140°F) and drop the last 50 g (1¾ oz) of leaves in, turn off the heat and cover to infuse for an hour. Over a low heat, heat the oil back up to 60°C (140°F) then carefully process in a blender on high for 1 minute. Strain through a fine sieve and chill over an ice bath. The oil will keep for 3–4 days in the refrigerator.

The next day when the curd is set, gently spoon the cheese into two to four small cheese baskets to drain on a draining rack for a few hours or up to 24 hours, at room temperature. Kept in a covered container on a rack in the refrigerator, they will last 2–3 days but they are best eaten fresh as the curd will firm up due to the whey continuing to drain.

Tear the figs open from the stem to the base, but keep them in one piece. With the open side facing down, put them between two sheets of baking paper and roll them out flat. Flip them over and lay them flat with the jammy side facing up. Dress the fig liberally with the vincotto and olive oil, then season with salt and pepper. Carefully take the cheese out of the moulds and dust with the dried fig leaf — break them in half if you'd like. Place on top of the figs and dress with the fig leaf oil and more vincotto.

Serve with warm grilled bread to spread with the cheese and figs. A drizzle of honey is also a great way to enjoy them.

NOTE

The figs need to be bursting and jammy. If you are having trouble finding figs, grilled grapes and fig jam are also delicious, as are fresh pitted cherries.

Goat's cheese with mirin

In Sydney in 2021, I worked with Mat Lindsay and Chef Jeff at Poly, a small natural wine bar with a hearth and wood grill in Surry Hills. Around Christmas time, there was a liver pâté dish encased in a firm-set dashi jelly on the menu. Often one of my jobs was to make, demould and set the pâté in the jelly.

There would always be plenty at the start of the night, and then by the last few dockets we would be running low and would need to set them to be ready for the next day. It was summer, the kitchen was doubly hot from the temperature outside and from the grill inside. It would inevitably be a nightmare every time trying to unmould these large terrine logs of soft, buttery pâté then to set them in the jelly to form perfect and even rectangles after a busy shift. Frustrating at the time, I do think it is a delicious way to serve something like this and it takes a few lessons to figure out how to do it more efficiently.

It is much easier with a small cheese, as in this recipe. And with the flavours of tangy goat's cheese and sweet mirin working very well together, this is a beautiful way to serve cheese.

You will need a small stainless-steel mould that the cheese fits in with space for the jelly to envelop it. These are available at cooking and kitchen homeware stores, but a small glass jar can be substituted as long as the jelly can be slid out. You'll also need a blowtorch.

YIELD

Makes 2 small cheeses

INGREDIENTS

100 ml (3½ fl oz) Ogasawara mirin (see note)
50 ml (1¾ fl oz) water
peel of ½ orange
4 sancho peppers, lightly crushed
1 teaspoon rice wine vinegar or fresh lemon juice
2 × small lactic-set goat's cheeses (see page 80 for homemade) that will fit inside the mould — cow's, sheep's or a blend will also work, however, the tang from the goat's cheese with the sweet wine is what I like most
3 gold-leaf gelatine leaves

TO SERVE

apples, plums, nashi pear or crisp persimmon
crackers of your choice

METHOD

Put the mirin, water, orange peel and peppers in a small stainless-steel pot, and warm gently over low heat. Turn the heat off and let it sit for 5 minutes, then add the rice wine vinegar or lemon juice. Bloom the gelatine leaves in cold water for a few minutes until soft, then add to the liquid and strain.

In the base of the mould, pour the jelly to 5–8 mm (¼–½ in) high, put in the fridge to set, and leave the remaining jelly to cool but not set. Once the mould is set, take the cheese out and unwrap it. With a small blowtorch, gently lick the jelly with the flame to loosen it slightly. This helps the cheese to adhere to the jelly and will stop it floating when the rest of the jelly is added.

Put the cheese, top side down, on the loose jelly and reset in the fridge for 10 minutes.

Pour the rest of the liquid jelly over to fully encase the cheese evenly by 8–10 mm (¼–½ in), the same as the bottom. If the jelly has set before you can pour it in, gently melt it, but don't pour it over hot as it will lift the set cheese from the base jelly when it melts. Leave to set for at least 90 minutes.

Using a blowtorch or warm water bath, gently loosen and demould the jelly onto a plate. Serve with fruit and crackers.

NOTE

Mirin is a type of rice wine similar to sake but with a lower alcohol content. For this cheese to be delicious, the mirin needs to be of high quality. Ogasawara mirin is handmade in Aichi, Japan, with high-quality glutinous rice and rice koji and no added sweeteners to give it a delicate and mild sweet umami flavour. If you are unable to find a similar-quality mirin, try a sweeter, low-alcohol artisan-style sake.

Fromage blanc and jam doughnut

Everybody loves a doughnut.

During the lockdown in Sydney during the pandemic in late 2021, I was fortunate enough to continue to make cheese for people to cook and enjoy in their homes. We had just moved to Sydney and into our apartment when the city was thrown into a closure that lasted nearly 4 months. As I had just started at Poly with Mat Lindsay, he allowed me to work in the Poly kitchen to make the cheese that I had been honing at home. His business partner and baker buddy, Dougal Muffet, was also at a loose end, stuck with his beautiful wheat, grains, pastries and breads and nowhere to sell them.

When the cheese took off and people got excited, we thought it would make sense for us to combine the bread and cheese for people enjoy at home during such difficult times. Every day, when people would come to pick up their cheese and bread, we would increase the offering, pushing each other and adding things to the sales to keep people interested and, more importantly, keep ourselves creative. They were some of the best times in the worst times.

Dougal made a bombolone, I made some cheese, and we combined the two into a plum and fromage blanc (fresh white cheese) bombolone. We had a hit.

While these doughnuts are not quite the same, they are delicious as is, or can be stuffed with all sorts of creams, custards, chocolates, jams and of course, fresh cheese.

The doughnut recipe is adapted from Justin Gellatly and St John restaurant in London.

You will need to start the doughnuts and mousse the day before.

YIELD

Makes 10 doughnuts

INGREDIENTS

1 litre (34 fl oz/4 cups) cottonseed or vegetable oil, for frying
80 g (2¾ oz) sugar
20 g (¾ oz) Whey powder (page 112) (optional)

FROMAGE BLANC MOUSSE

1½ gold-strength gelatine leaves, soaked in cold water
½ vanilla bean
85 ml (2¾ fl oz) pouring (single/light) cream
35 g (1¼ oz) sugar
zest of ½ lemon
175 g (6 oz) fresh white cheese (for homemade see page 48), hung to the consistency of labneh (see notes)
85 g (3 oz) cultured cream (for homemade see page 56) (see notes)

DOUGHNUT DOUGH

4 g (⅛ oz) dried yeast
75 ml (2½ fl oz) milk at 37°C (98.6°F)/body temperature
zest of ½ lemon
30 g (1 oz) sugar
250 g (9 oz/1⅔ cups) strong white flour
pinch of salt
2 eggs
60 g (2 oz) soft butter

METHOD

To make the fromage blanc mousse, soak the gelatine leaves in cold water and scrape the seeds out of the vanilla bean.

In a small saucepan, warm the first 85 g (3 oz) of cream, the sugar and the scraped vanilla seeds. Add the scraped pod too to get all the vanilla from it, but take it out and discard once infused. Stir to melt the sugar as it is warming so it doesn't catch, then turn off the heat. Add the bloomed gelatine and mix it through, then transfer to a medium-sized bowl and allow to cool for a few minutes.

Whisk the fresh white cheese for 1-2 minutes to loosen until smooth, then add the cream mix and incorporate well.

Whisk the cultured cream to soft peaks and fold it through the cheese mix with a whisk. Cover and refrigerate until set overnight.

The next day, place into a piping (icing) bag. If it is too stiff, whisk to soften, but it does need to be firm to stay inside the doughnut.

To make the doughnuts, combine the yeast with the milk to activate for 5 minutes.

Add the lemon zest to the sugar and rub together, then add to the flour and salt in a stand mixer fitted with a dough hook and start mixing on a low speed.

Beat the eggs lightly in a small bowl, then add to the flour mix gradually, about one egg amount at a time until incorporated. You may have to stop the mixer to scrape the side down.

Slowly add the soft butter, about 15 g (½ oz) at a time to incorporate and knead until smooth, glossy and very elastic

Lightly grease a bowl and store the dough, covered, in the refrigerator overnight.

The next day, roll the dough in 50 g (1¾ oz) balls and prove on a lightly floured tray lined with baking paper for 3–4 hours until puffy..

Heat the oil in a large stainless-steel saucepan to 175–185°C (345–165°F). The dough balls are very fragile and soft at this stage so gently pick each doughnut up and gently lower one at a time into the oil. Fry them for a minute or two on each side, being careful not to overcrowd the pot. Flip them often so as not to colour them too much and keep the oil at the right temperature. If the oil is too low, the doughnuts will become greasy and oily; too high and they will get too browned.

When they are ready, lift them out with a slotted spoon. Drain them lightly on paper towel and allow to cool for 1 hour.

Mix the sugar and whey powder (if using) together, then toss the doughnuts in the mix and return to the draining rack. If they are still hot and oily when they are coated, the sugar mix will dissolve and become greasy.

Make a small slit in the side of each doughnut, and pipe in the mousse, jam, chocolate or whatever you'd like. Squeeze the filling in until you feel the doughnut blow up, but not too much as the filling will ooze back out. If the jam or other filling isn't pipeable, give it a whisk prior to loosen it slightly before piping. Dust with more sugar if needed.

NOTES

Yoghurt, ricotta or other soft curd cheese are all good substitutes.

Pouring (single/light) cream also works, I just like the added tang from the cultured cream, and it firms up the mousse more.

Sussex pond — lamb fat pudding and clotted cream

In early Spring 2020, I visited Tom and Maddie Wilde and their family at their sheep cheese farm, Cambray, in Nannup, Western Australia, to spend a few days with them on the property, learning about their farmstead cheese operation during the busy lambing season.

Lambing for sheep, kidding for goats and calving for cows is a busy time of the year when the herd is giving birth and the farmers are very busy assisting, caring for strugglers and ensuring the animals are all looked after. As the field is overrun with lambs, the milk is being collected in the sheds and then being turned into cheese in the dairy. It is quite a spectacle to witness, and understand just how hard sheep faming and cheesemaking is.

After spending time with the team, milking and being in the room making cheese, Tom gifted me some lamb suet, which is the hard fat around the loin and kidneys.

I took it back with me to Mum's place in Perth and we had suet pudding with apple, rhubarb and cream for dinner. Tart rhubarb and apples, moist, soft pastry and sweet syrup with rich cream — damn it was good.

Beef suet is generally used in savoury and sweet pastry applications, particularly in English cookery, and especially for Christmas pudding. It should be available from a good butcher.

The puddings do take a while to steam, around 2—3 hours, but once they are cooked they can be kept in the steamer until ready to be served.

YIELD

Makes 5—6 puddings

EQUIPMENT

you will need 6 small stainless-steel or aluminium pudding moulds about 7.5 cm (3 in) — the puddings can also be made in small glass jars, but size and cooking time may vary

INGREDIENTS

- 100 g (3½ oz) suet (preferably beef as lamb fat can have too strong a flavour), cleaned of any sinew
- 40 g (1½ oz) butter, cold and diced
- 165 g (6 oz) plain (all-purpose) flour + extra for dusting
- ¾ teaspoon baking powder
- pinch of sea salt flakes
- 1 egg yolk
- 1 tablespoon milk
- 80 g (2¾ oz) butter, at room temperature
- 80 g (2¾ oz) raw (demerara) sugar
- seeds scraped from 1 vanilla bean, or ¼ teaspoon vanilla bean paste
- 1 bunch of rhubarb — 180 g (6½ oz) diced, rest of bunch reserved
- 60 g (2 oz) Bravo apple, skin on, diced (see note)
- 1 Meyer lemon
- 150 g (5½ oz) sugar + extra as needed
- clotted cream (for homemade see page 56) to serve

Stuff the pudding.

Seal the pudding. If it tears, squash it back together.

METHOD

If you get the suet from a butcher, ask them to mince (grind) it for you, or you can do it yourself at home. Tear and shred it into little flecks if you do not have a mincer (grinder) and put the fat in the refrigerator to cool with the butter.

In a food processor, pulse the cold butter and suet together with the sifted flour, baking powder and salt until a crumb forms. Whisk the egg and milk together in a bowl, add to the butter mixture and pulse to bring the dough together.

On a floured bench, knead the dough until it comes together into a ball, then wrap and refrigerate.

Cream the butter and sugar together with the vanilla in a stand mixer or with electric beaters and set aside.

Wash and trim the rhubarb and, using the smaller inner stems, cut into 1 cm (½ in) pieces reserving the rest and any peel and trimmings, as you will have plenty left over from a bunch.

Dice the apple a little larger, about 1.5 cm (½ in), then toss it into the creamed butter mix with 80 g (2¾ oz) of the rhubarb. Keep any apple cores and trimmings to be used later.

Slice half the lemon into fifths, or slices about 4 mm (¼ in) thick, then poach them in 250 ml (8½ fl oz/ 1 cup) water with 50 g (1¾ oz) of the white sugar for 3–4 minutes.

Take the dough out of the fridge and divide into five to six equal-sized balls, about 65–75 g (2¼–2¾ oz) each depending on the mould size.

Butter the moulds and lightly flour them, then press the dough into each so they are about 3–5 mm (⅛–¼ in) thick with overhanging pastry to close them once filled. They will tear and break but that's okay — just press them back together.

Smooth it over gently with your thumb.

Ready to share.

Place a tablespoon or so of the rhubarb mix into the mould, then squish the lemon slice in and top with another tablespoon of mixture so it sits just below the lip of the mould. Seal the pudding tightly and cover with a round of baking paper, then tightly wrap in foil.

In a simmering steamer, steam the puddings for 2–3 hours, constantly topping up the water in the base as needed. If you don't want to steam them all, you can freeze them and steam at another time.

While the puddings are steaming, place the remaining 100 g (3½ oz) rhubarb in a pot with the apple trimmings and cover with water. Bring to the boil and cook for 10 minutes. Strain, add the remaining white sugar and continue cooking until you have a syrup. Cool, then squeeze the rest of the Meyer lemon juice in.

Cut the rest of the bunch of rhubarb the same size, toss with 5% of its weight in sugar and cook down in a saucepan to a compote, then cool and refrigerate. (Serve this with the finished pudding and serve any leftovers for breakfast with yoghurt.)

Once the puddings are cooked, gently remove them from the moulds with a paring knife and serve with the compote and the clotted cream.

NOTE

Bravo apples are a dark burgundy red coloured apple that were developed in Donnybrook, Western Australia, not far from Cambray Cheese. They are crisp, delicious apples that are sweet with a mild acidity, and they don't brown quickly when cut. You can substitute another sweet apple in their place.

Goat's curd brûlée

Fresh goat's curd has often been thought of as savoury and a cheese to have at the start of a meal or with a beetroot (beet) salad. However, I like the tang and subtleness it can add to a crème brûlée.

For this recipe, it is best to make the mix the day before to allow it to settle — this gives you a beautiful silky texture.

YIELD

Serves 3–4

INGREDIENTS

vanilla bean
zest of ¼ lemon + extra to serve
40 g (1½ oz) sugar
200 ml (7 fl oz) pouring (single/light) cream
160 g (5½ oz) goat's curd (for homemade see page 60) or goat's fromage frais — fresh yoghurt texture; too thick and the brûlée will be dense
7 egg yolks
iced water
boiling water
sea salt flakes

METHOD

Scrape the vanilla bean and add the seeds to a bowl with the lemon zest and sugar. Lightly rub the mixture, using your fingertips, to combine.

Combine half the sugar mix, the cream and the scraped vanilla pod in a pot over a low heat and dissolve the sugar. Once hot, add the goat's cheese and gently mix through with a whisk until smooth and incorporated. Discard the vanilla pod.

Add the rest of the sugar into the yolks with a pinch of salt, whisk together, then slowly pour a small amount of the hot cream into the yolks and mix. Return all the mixture back into the pot. Over a low heat, stir the custard constantly until slightly thickened, about 1 minute — no more or the brûlée won't set when baked.

Strain immediately, cool over an ice bath, then refrigerate overnight. This helps to give the brûlée a beautiful silky texture.

The next day, preheat the oven to 125°C (257°F), bring the mix to room temperature, weigh it and divide it into three small, flat bowls. Lay a towel in the base of a deep tray and set the bowls on top. Gently pour boiling water in until about halfway up the sides of the bowls, then place on the middle rack of the oven. Cook for 35–40 minutes or until just set with is a slight wobble in the middle. Take them out, let them cool, cover and refrigerate.

When ready, cover with a thin layer of sugar. Brûlée (caramelise) the top using a blowtorch. Season with a pinch of sea salt and fresh lemon zest.

Serve, crack the top and eat immediately.

If you're feeling fancy, an Amarena or brandied cherry on top is a delight.

White cheese, black sesame and strawberry mousse cake

My older sister Ali is adamant that a cheesecake has to have a biscuit base. I don't agree. The more cheese the better and, in this case, it's about the creamy cheese, nutty sesame flavour and the sweet strawberries.

Once upon a time, I worked with an Irish chef called JP, who made the most delicious strawberry jelly and coconut sorbet dessert. The steeping of the strawberries made such a beautiful perfume that would permeate the kitchen, and whenever I smell a ripe, juicy strawberry I think of him and that jelly.

The texture of cooked strawberries is not pleasant, but drying them after the syrup is made keeps that beautiful flavour in. It also gives them a nice chew, which works well in place of a biscuit base among all the fresh cheese. It is quite decadent, so I would recommend sharing.

You will need two 9 cm (3½ in) diameter, 3 cm (1¼ in) deep cookie cutters, cake ring moulds or something similar to build them in.

YIELD

Makes 2 — to share between 4

INGREDIENTS

¼ teaspoon powdered gelatine
30 ml (1 fl oz) pouring (single/light) cream
200 g (7 oz) fresh white cheese (for homemade see page 48), drained to the consistency of cream cheese, thicker than labneh at room temperature
40 g (1½ oz) sugar
salt
90 g (3 oz) thick (double/heavy) cream at room temperature
1-1.5 tablespoons organic black sesame paste

FOR THE STRAWBERRIES
250 g (9 oz) ripe strawberries
25 g (1 oz) caster (superfine) sugar
1 tablespoon muscatel vinegar (see note)

METHOD

For the strawberries, wash and destem them, cut in half if large, and place in a stainless-steel bowl. Toss with the sugar, cover tightly, and set over a simmering pot of water for 1 hour. Cook them gently, as you don't want them to go to mush. Remove from the heat, uncover and cool. Gently take the strawberries out and strain, reserving the liquid in the refrigerator. Lay the strawberries out on a drying rack and dehydrate in a low oven or dehydrator at 85°C (185°F) for 3–4 hours. They should be gummy but not crisp or dry. Rotate and flip them every hour or so, dipping back in the syrup before continuing to dry.

In a small saucepan, bloom the powdered gelatine with the cold pouring cream for a minute. Over a low heat, gently warm to melt and set aside to cool slightly.

Using a hand mixer, whip the cheese until light and fluffy, about a minute or two, then beat in the sugar and salt to taste. Loosen the double cream and then whisk in with the cheese to fully incorporate.

Line a small, flat tray with baking paper and set the moulds on top. Lightly grease and line each ring mould with baking paper around the circumference.

Once the pouring cream mix is at room temperature, fold through the cheese, mix until smooth, then refrigerate for 10 minutes to firm up slightly.

Lay the strawberries in prior to filling.

Gently fold the tahini through to create the swirl, or mix it thoroughly.

Place enough mousse into the base of each mould to just cover it, about 1 cm (½ in) high. This prevents the sesame from running when the mould comes off. Lightly fold the sesame into the rest of mousse, and put a small amount in each mould. Lay five to six strawberries, depending on size, over the mousse and lightly press in. Gently cover with the rest of the mousse to fill. Cover and refrigerate for 6–8 hours or until set.

When ready to serve, take the strawberry liquid and season with the muscatel vinegar to taste. It should be just present to balance the sweetness but not sharp. Use a small knife to gently release the cakes into small bowls and pour the strawberry juice around them to form a pool.

NOTE

A quality sherry vinegar can be substituted for the muscatel vinegar.

White cheese, black sesame and strawberry mousse cake

I heart mango & cheese ... and raspberries

I heart mango & cheese ... and raspberries

Coeur a la crème is a cheese dessert that originates from Anjou, France. Usually made with fromage blanc (fresh white cheese) and served with raspberries, it is typically made in a ceramic perforated dish in the shape of a heart (coeur).

I absolutely love fresh mango, especially with fresh cheese. Luckily, Australia produces some of the best mangoes in the world and it can be a real treat to pick up a whole tray from a farmer on the side of the road on long road trips in the country — although as my wife Andrea can attest, sometimes you might get more mangoes than you bargain for.

You will also need heart-shaped perforated moulds, or you can use other shapes or cheese hoops as the cheese does need to be drained as it sets. You will also need a kitchen blowtorch.

YIELD

If you are using small heart-shaped moulds, about 11 cm (4¼ in) this recipe will serve 2; 1 larger round mould at 16 cm (6¼ in) will serve 4

INGREDIENTS

- 250 g (9 oz) fresh white cheese (for homemade see page 48)
- 130 g (4½ oz) caster (superfine) sugar + extra to serve
- juice of ½ lemon
- 2 egg whites
- 180 ml (6 fl oz) pouring (single/light) cream
- pinch of sea salt flakes
- 2 firm, ripe mangoes

CARAMEL

- 80 g (2¾ oz/⅓ cup) caster (superfine) sugar

METHOD

Cut and wet some cheesecloth with enough overhang to cover the moulds once filled.

In a small bowl, whisk the cheese with 40 g (1½ oz) of the sugar until smooth, then add the lemon juice.

In a bowl, whisk the egg white with a pinch of salt to firm peaks, then slowly add another 40 g (1½ oz) of the sugar and continue whipping till glossy.

In another bowl, lightly whip the cream to soft peaks. Fold the whipped cream into the cheese mix well, then very gently fold the egg whites through using a whisk. Pour the mix into the mould/s to fill, then cover with the cheesecloth. Fill the mould/s right up. Refrigerate to set for at least 4 hours depending on the size of the mould/s. If larger it may need more time.

While the mixture is setting, take the cheeks of the mango and peel them, keeping as much natural shape as possible. If the mango is too ripe and soft, this may be difficult.

Put the pit and peels (approximately 500 g/1 lb 2 oz) in a saucepan with the remaining 50 g (1¾ oz) sugar. Mash the pit and peels, then add 300 ml (10 fl oz) of water and bring to a simmer. Cook for 25 minutes, then strain.

In another saucepan, make a dry caramel with the 80 g (2¾ oz) of sugar, cooked until dark (about 180°C/356°F), then very carefully pour the mango syrup in. It will steam and spit so do it under an exhaust fan. Allow to cool.

Mango layers, cut, spread and shape before being slid onto the cream.

Use the best raspberries for presentation and the rest for the sauce.

To serve, invert the cream onto a serving plate. With a sharp paring knife, take the mango cheeks and thinly slice them, using the tip of the knife and your finger to manoeuvre the slices into fans and shapes to fill the top of the heart-shaped cheese. It is quite finicky, so it may take you a few attempts. Once the mango is in place, refrigerate for 10 minutes to firm up again before lightly sprinkling the mango slices with sugar. With a blowtorch, brûlée the sugar to a crust and allow to set.

Drizzle the caramel over the top and serve.

For a raspberry version, purée 250 g (9 oz) of raspberries in a blender with 20 g (¾ oz) of sugar and a squeeze of lemon juice, then strain. Dot the cheese with 250 g (9 oz) fresh raspberries, then pour the syrup over and dust with icing (confectioners') sugar.

New York cheesecake with passionfruit and yoghurt cream

Cakes are often associated with birthdays in my family, and we didn't really do cake outside of that. When I arrived back home from New York, I experimented and cooked so much in Mum's little home kitchen that the two of us put on quite a bit of weight. We had dessert and watched TV every night together. It was a really fun time and the most time we had shared since I had left Perth in 2007.

A New York cheesecake is dense, rich, decadent and slightly firm, unlike a regular cheesecake, which is light and fluffy. Here, it's all about the cream cheese, which provides the richness, tang and texture.

YIELD

Makes 12–16 slices

INGREDIENTS

145 g (5 oz) Granita (sweet wholemeal) biscuits
85 g (3 oz) butter, melted + extra for greasing
200 g (7 oz) caster (superfine) sugar + 2 extra tablespoons
750 g (1 lb 11 oz/3 cups) cream cheese (for homemade see page 64)
6 g (⅛ oz) sea salt flakes
seeds scraped from 1 vanilla bean
3 eggs + 1 egg white for brushing
120 g (4½ oz) crème fraîche (for homemade see page 56)
120 g (4½ oz) thick (double/heavy) cream
80 g (2¾ oz) edible hibiscus blossoms, dried
300 ml (10 fl oz) pouring (single/light) cream
100 g (3½ oz) yoghurt
fresh passionfruit, to serve

METHOD

Let the cream cheese, eggs, crème fraîche and cream come to room temperature, which will allow them to mix well for a smooth, even-textured cake.

In a food processor, blitz the biscuits to a fine crumb. Add the melted butter and 1 tablespoon of the sugar, then mix to form a dough.

Grease a 20 cm (8 in) springform mould and line the base and side with greaseproof paper. Press the crumb into the mould evenly and bake at 190°C (375°F) for 10-12 minutes. Remove from the oven, brush with egg white and let cool.

In a stand mixer or with electric beaters, beat the cream cheese and sugar for 3–5 minutes until smooth. Add the salt, vanilla and eggs, one at a time, scraping down the sides after each addition.

Whip the crème fraîche slightly to soften it, then add it to the mix. Do the same with the thick cream then fold it through to incorporate well.

Pour the mix into the mould and cover with foil. Place the cake in a deep roasting tin on top of a towel and carefully pour boiling water in to come two-thirds of the way up the side of the mould. On the middle shelf in the oven, bake the cake at 190°C (375°F) for 30 minutes, then reduce the heat to 165°C (330°F) and bake for a further hour. Check the cake with a skewer and remove from the oven once done. Depending on your oven, this make take longer. Remove from the oven once ready, carefully take the foil off and allow to cool completely, then refrigerate for at least 6 hours – overnight is better.

When ready, undo the mould by running a hot knife around the edge and discard the paper. Completely unmould the cheesecake from the base by inverting it onto a baking paper–lined disc or large plate. Remove the base paper before flipping back over onto your serving dish.

In a blinder, blitz the dried hibiscus to a fine powder.

Whip the pouring cream to soft peaks with the final tablespoon of sugar, then add the yoghurt and whip again to soft peaks and place in a piping (icing) bag.

Pipe the yoghurt cream onto the cake and dust with the hibiscus powder. Cut into wedges and serve with fresh passionfruit.

The cheese *plate*

I feel that there are no real right and wrong pairings with cheese. That's part of the joy of cheese for me — there are thousands of different styles from all over the world and it is exciting and interesting to play around with them and other ingredients to make for a tasty plate of cheese.

You could use cheese you've made yourself, or quality cheese that you've bought. The combinations, accoutrements, presentation and styles are endless. Seasonality plays an important role in not just the milk and cheese but also what is served with your cheese.

Going to the market is a huge source of inspiration for me, not only for cooking but with my cheesemaking and preserving too. It is a great opportunity to see and taste unusual and exciting produce and ingredients that you wouldn't normally see. Loquats, Hachiya persimmons, nettles, spring garlic, blood and greengage plums, and old heirloom varieties of apples and green zebra tomatoes are just some of the beautiful items that go with cheese, which you won't see in a supermarket.

Some people flat out say, 'I don't do goat's cheese or blue cheese'. Maybe they don't like a fresh barnyard or chalky goat's cheese, or strong and dry blue cheese, but perhaps an aged Spanish goat's cheese or raw milk Stichelton might change their minds. I like to visit different cheese shops and try new cheeses all the time. I have my favourite types but there are always new ones to taste and explore in the cabinet; it's what makes cheese so interesting. Very much like wine, there are hundreds of words used to describe the complexities, profiles, aromas and flavours of cheese. Use your senses when you are tasting — smell the cheese, take your time and appreciate the mouthfeel, flavours and aromas that you are picking up. Find ones you like.

This chapter covers some important things to consider when designing your cheese plate, as well as a few delicious recipes for accompaniments.

Choosing cheese

What cheese do you like to eat and what cheese do you think your guests like to eat? A safe bet is a mixture of cheese — perhaps a soft, white mould style, a grassy semi-hard and a savoury blue cheese. This is a pretty classic and simple selection that caters for all tastes. Some more ideas:

- RAW MILK CHEESE PLATE A plate of cheeses made from raw milk, to celebrate the diversity and contribution to cheese that raw milk gives us.
- MILK TYPE A plate of cheese from one type of milk — a sheep's milk plate of Brebirousse d'Argental, Roquefort and Ossau-Iraty, for example.
- BLUE CHEESE PLATE A selection of local and international cheeses. This could include the classics Roquefort, Gorgonzola and Valdeón. Or it could be a selection of Gorgonzola Dolce and Piccante in their varying states of age and texture.
- REGIONAL CHEESE PLATE With the growth of artisan cheese, there are many local cheeses being made, and visiting regional areas where dairy and cheese are produced can provide opportunities to use a single area, state or nation's cheese for your cheese board. In New York, pioneering cheese legend Anne Saxelby created Saxelby's, a cheese shop that celebrates All-American artisan cheese, and there are now some restaurants in Australia offering a full selection of Australian cheese on their menus. Your cheesemonger will be able to help you select a range of cheese from a certain region or place.
- MATURATION PLATE Some cheese is available in different stages of maturation and this can be an interesting way of serving cheese. You could also do this with cheese you have made yourself, and taste the differing textures, flavours and aromas of cheese at different stages.
- HOUSEMADE PLATE Your own cheese!

How much cheese should you serve?

That depends on how many styles and when and where in the meal you plan to serve the cheese, and also what with. Choose your cheese first and then go from there. If you are serving five varieties you will need less of each than if you were only to serve three styles.

If it's for snacking at a picnic with other small things, 60-75 g (2–2¾ oz) of cheese might suffice. After a dinner party meal, before dessert, maybe 25-30 g (1 oz) per person. And if it's for watching a movie with friends maybe 85-100 g (3–3½ oz) per person will be just right.

When you are deciding what cheese you'd like to serve, think about how much you think your guests may eat, then aim a little higher. A little extra left over for the next day isn't a bad thing.

Seasonality and cheese

As mentioned earlier in the book, cheesemakers work with the seasons. Spring and summer is the time for soft sheep's and goat's cheese, autumn is for washed-rind and bark-wrapped cheese, while the harder styles of cheese, due to their longer maturation, are generally available year-round. The seasons and the milk composition change, therefore the cheese is also changing, with some cheese only available when the cheesemaker has the best milk — as is the case for Rogue River Blue.

Good cheese is expensive and by now you will have realised the amount of work, effort, transport and manufacturing costs that go into making cheese. You might want to consider that when building your cheese plate too — a nice mix of imported and local cheese will provide you with good cheese but not blow the budget.

What to put on the plate

In all honesty, I think a perfect wedge, slice or piece of perfectly made, matured and tempered cheese is all you need.

Fresh, fermented, dried, pickled, baked and well-grown things are a welcome addition to the plate too. I also like to make and find unusual things and try them with the cheese I make and serve.

Cheese, with its fermented and deep flavours and aromas, lends itself to other funky and wild things and, when paired well, can they complement and lift each other. Wine, beer, cider and other beverages often go well with cheese, but sometimes not. A good rule of thumb for this is what grows together, goes together — you will know what that means if you have indulged in the unbeatable combination of Vin Jaune and Comté, both from the Jura region — a truly perfect marriage. If you haven't, you must.

Other things that you may not consider can also work. Chocolate is fermented cocoa and pairs with milk in hot chocolate; coffee beans are fermented coffee cherries that are also paired with fresh milk, when brewed.

My friend Caroline Hesse once told me about cheese and coffee hour at the now-closed Crown Finish Caves in Brooklyn. It seemed odd to me at the time but, the more I thought about it, and having once being a latte drinker, the more sense it made. Coffee and milk — what a revelation! Even more so when the team at Crown Finish Caves aged cow's and goat's surface-ripened cheese with coffee grounds, a specialty they called Coffee Cloud Heights. This led me to use dried used coffee grounds on some of my cheese as well as in crackers to pair with cheese.

Chocolate goes well with the younger, fresher styles. Fresh goat's cheese works well with chocolate in ganache form; a more aged variety might work better with a nut chocolate, and blue cheese with a good couverture dark chocolate. Wine and chocolate works, so does cheese and chocolate. With this in mind, think and play around with combinations with cheese. The cheese world is your oyster, so find the pearls.

The acidity, sweetness, variety, age and texture of cheese can impact how they pair with certain things too. The really deep, caramel, salty, fudge-like notes that come from some alpine cheeses love tropical fruit. Pineapple is a good example, especially when it is slowly dried and the sugars become more condensed. Raspberries, mulberries and other summer berries marry very well with rich, creamy young sheep's milk cheese and the bright, sharp tanginess of white mould ripened goat's cheese — they are also both In season at this time.

Stone fruit and mango are also delicious with fresh cheese. Quality dried organic stone fruit pairs well with firmer styles of cheese from the previous year's summer of cheesemaking.

As the seasons change, so to do the cheeses served, with pickles, onions, potatoes and preserves coming out to go with washed-rinds, bark-wrapped cheeses, baked cheese and blues.

Depending on where you are and what season it is, farmhouse cheesemakers quite often have orchards, nut trees and other edible plants on their properties. They make their own condiments to go with their cheese and will probably have some good ideas about what to pair with them.

Travel, experience and tradition also play a part in putting things together and connecting the dots. Seeking out the best of something is highly recommended. A beautiful Freddy Guy hazelnut from Oregon, bursting with flavour, is worth putting on a cheese plate. A generic, chemically produced hazelnut from the supermarket most definitely will not have the same taste or effect.

Definitely put as much effort and thought into sourcing and making your accoutrements as you do into sourcing and making your cheese. Some cheese is best left to shine by itself, so don't over-complicate things if they don't need it. Some things just work so well together, others might need some thinking.

Dried soda fruits

If you are making whey sodas with fruit, keep the fermented fruit and dry it once the soda is ready. For the firmer fruits and vegetables, you may need to poach them before drying.

Carefully lay the fruit out on racks and dehydrate at 75°C (170°F) in a slow oven or dehydrator for about 4–6 hours, depending on the fruit, size, texture and how chewy or crisp you want them. Berries are delicious with fresher, younger cheeses and, in desserts, pineapple and orange are really good with alpine-style cheese, and figs and cherries with blue cheese.

When drying, make sure the pieces are laid flat and spread apart, so they dry slowly and evenly.

INGREDIENTS

500 ml (17 fl oz/2 cups) water
150 g (5½ oz) sugar
150 ml (5 fl oz) glucose syrup
250 g (9 oz) pineapple or other dried fruit, peeled and cut into even 3 cm (1¼ in) pieces

METHOD

Bring the water, sugar and glucose syrup to the boil, then poach the pineapple until just cooked and let it cool in the syrup. Dry the fruit on racks in a low oven or dehydrator at 85–90°C (185–195°F) for 3-4 hours until chewy. Keep in an airtight container in the refrigerator.

Soda fruit jams

If you are juicing or blending fruit for your sodas, keep the pulp after straining from the soda base. Whole apples are good for this because of the high pectin. Cook the pulp out with sugar, spices or whatever you like, and finish with a little lemon juice, vinegar or citric acid. Cool and serve with cheese, stuff into doughnuts or dollop on pancakes.

Hoshigaki – dried persimmons

Hoshigaki are available in specialty stores in dried form but making them yourself is much more fun.

I've seen some creative chefs and people making these with other fruits and vegetables but, for this recipe, use firm, unripened Hayachi persimmons, preferably ones with the stem on so you can tie and hang them. If not, a small screw can be inserted.

These fruits come into season in early autumn. As they are really astringent in this state, they need drying or ripening until they are mushy. When they are dried in this Japanese fashion, they become quite jammy and are delicious with cheese.

First carefully trim around the top in a circular motion, being careful not to take too much off and leaving the stem on. Peel the whole fruit and tie the stem or screw with twine.

Hang them inside where they won't be disturbed, somewhere not too warm or too dark, with space between them for a good amount of air circulation. After a few days, the surface should start to dry out, so gently massage each one to release the sugars and continue drying. Keep massaging them every 2–3 days until they are coated with a sugary mildew. Keep drying them until they feel like a dried apricot or similar, anywhere between 3–5 weeks depending on the environment.

Take them down, remove the string (and screw if present) and gently roll before storing in an airtight container.

Grilled grapes

Dried, shrivelled grapes are not my jam at all. In my opinion, if you're going to serve grapes with cheese, use them fresh or, even better, gently blister them on a grill and toss with a muscatel vinegar, olive oil, sea salt flakes and pepper to eat with a homemade fresh soft cheese. But if you do like muscatels, try making your own or sourcing a quality one.

Grilled stone fruit is also very good with fresher styles of cheese, macerated in a little champagne or prosecco. Serve with fresh white cheese (for homemade see page 48), ricotta, mascarpone or similar cheeses.

Nuts

As mentioned before, look for small farms and people cultivating things in a small, caring way. A really good nut is something that can be delicious with cheese. Macadamias, walnuts, pecans, Brazil nuts, hazelnuts and almonds are all delicious lightly roasted and seasoned with sea salt flakes, spices and a touch of sugar.

Beetroot stalk marmalade

This is a tip that I learned in kitchens in New York where we had excess vegetable offcuts, ends and scraps. When buying beetroot, keep the stalks and wash them thoroughly before making this marmalade. It's good with fresher goat's, blue cheese and even steak. It's also excellent with dark chocolate. Other vegetable stalks, leaves and trimmings can also make a good condiment for cheese in this manner.

YIELD

Makes 100 g (3½ oz)

INGREDIENTS

100 g (3½ oz) beetroot (beet) stalks — about 1 bunch worth if baby beetroot
extra-virgin olive oil
30 g (1 oz) raw (demerara) or brown sugar
50 ml (1¾ fl oz) red wine vinegar
freshly ground black pepper
orange zest

METHOD

Finely slice the beetroot stalks straight across, then slowly cook them down with a splash of olive oil in a saucepan over medium heat for about 5 minutes. Add the sugar and cook for a further 5 minutes, then add the vinegar and gently cook down until slightly thickened. Season with pepper, salt and a little orange zest. Store in an airtight container in the refrigerator for up to 3 months.

Loquat paste

Loquats are a subtropical evergreen shrub native to China and bear white, sweet-scented flowers and bright, aromatic, yellow to orange fruit in spring. Also known as Japanese medlar and similar in shape to a prune, with one to three seeds inside, they can be eaten freshly peeled or used in jams, jellies and preserves.

YIELD

Makes 400-450 g (14 oz–1 lb)

INGREDIENTS

500 g (1 lb 2 oz) ripe loquats, bright orange and yellow (see note)
375 g (13 oz) sugar
juice and zest of ½ lemon

METHOD

Wash the loquats and place in a wide-bottomed pot so they are in a single layer. Cover with water and simmer until soft, about 30 minutes. Strain and pass the fruit through a mouli (food mill) or strainer to remove the seeds and peels.

Return the puree to the pot over medium heat and slowly add the sugar, ½ cup at a time, stirring to incorporate it all. Add the lemon juice and zest and bring to a slow boil. Keep cooking, stirring to prevent it from catching, for a further 30–35 minutes, or until you can drag a spoon through it, and it stays separated.

Pour into a lined mould and allow to completely cool. Store in an airtight container.

NOTE

This recipe also works with pink guava, but make sure they are ripe and aromatic and cut into quarters before bringing to the boil — the seeds and peels should also be milled out in the same way.

Loquat paste. Keep it in the pantry and serve with cheese.

Crackers vs. bread vs. toast

The way I see it is, it's all about the cheese. You want to highlight and complement it, not mask it, and a meal that has multiple servings of bread can be a bit much. That said, a warm, torn baguette with a wheel of soft cheese or wedge of sharp cheddar is a very good lunch. But choose your starch wisely.

Thinking about what cheese you have, where it is served in the meal and the condiments you are serving it with, can help you decide what else to serve it with. The thickness of a cracker should be considered — a thin cracker with a thick hunk of cheese may be a bit finicky and shatter at the first bite. Choose something that is going to do the job.

A fresher style of curd could go with crackers, fresh bread or toast; a delicate and rich white mould suits a cracker or fresh bread; and something a bit bolder could handle the char of toast. Mind you, an overripe white mould cheese in a grilled cheese sandwich isn't the worst idea either.

WILDFLOWER

CHAPTER 10

A few things to *finish*

By now, hopefully you have a bit more of an understanding of how cheese is made, how to select it, how to cook with it and how to eat it.

This last chapter is going to tie things up — or should I say 'wrap them up'. If you're not into cheese puns, you are going to need to start getting used to it, as the cheese world and people who work in it have hundreds of them and are not shy about sharing them.

The following pages contain a few final tips, quips and advice on everything thus far.

Buying cheese

Just like you would go to a quality butcher, fishmonger, market or fruit and veg purveyor for those items, you really ought to go to a good cheesemonger, cheese shop or farmhouse to get your cheese. Here are a few reasons why:

- Good cheesemongers have relationships with their cheesemakers. They know what is happening on the farm, with the milk and with the cheese. Some even hand-pick the cheese for their shop.
- They have intimate knowledge of the cheeses in their cabinet.
- Some may have even miked the animal, then made, aged the cheese before serving it to you.
- Buying cheese from a cheesemonger supports smaller, local artisan cheesemakers and businesses.
- They can tell you what is best to eat at the moment – cheese has seasonality, and a cheesemonger knows when to eat what and when.
- When cooking, a cheesemonger will be able to help you choose what cheese and ripeness is best for what you are using it for.
- Get to know your cheesemonger, and they'll get to know what you like and also introduce you to new cheeses they think you'll like.
- Cheese cut to order is the best way to buy cheese.
- Your cheese should be wrapped and stored well.
- Cheesemongers know how to have fun.

Finding a good cheesemonger is a bit like a dating – find one that has the qualities you like, tells you romantic stories, has time for you, gives you their best and helps create memories.

Learn the history and speak the truth

Cheese has history, and cheese isn't just milk. Cheese and cheesemaking has evolved over thousands of years so the least we can do is learn the origins, the stories the traditions and the history of what we are eating and serving. There is a real romance to cheese and the stories are often fascinating and bring purpose to the cheese.

If you are putting cheese on the menu, learn about it, study it, eat it, enjoy it and educate others.

It is frustrating to see cheese mislabelled and misrepresented on menus. The cheese has often been around for thousands of years and may even be a DPO or AOP protected cheese that has gone through strict production controls and regulations for it to be called by a certain name, or it could be a new cheese being made from a new producer coming into the market.

As the final link between production and consumption, markets, cheesemongers, chefs and restaurants should get it right. It's also okay not to know – just make sure you find out and keep questioning and learning.

Serving cheese

Table cheese should be served at the correct temperature. You are really doing the cheese and cheesemaker a disservice by serving a beautiful cheese stone cold. Like wine, it needs time to open up and reveal its flavours, textures and aromas.

This is easier in a home setting. Pull a soft cheese out an hour or two before serving, and a harder style cheese out a few hours prior, depending on the ambient temperature. Unwrap it and let it breathe as if you were decanting a wine.

In a restaurant kitchen, this is more challenging. Pull out what you need and keep it somewhere where it's not going to dry out — a wooden wine box with a breather for airflow is a good idea. Cut the cheese to order if possible and trim off a little of the exposed piece as you go. Cover the cut side with cheese paper or towel before putting it back in the cheese cave. Baking paper allows the cheese to dry out quickly. Remember, cheese loves moisture. Taking cheese in and out of temperature too often isn't great for the cheese, so only have out what you need and replenish as needed. If in doubt, don't serve it.

Cutting cheese

Cheese ripens from the outside in — from the outer moulds and rinds to the inner cheese paste — as in white mould cheeses. Or, as in the case of cheddar, it can ripen from the inner cheese paste to the outer rinds. To get the full spectrum of flavour, texture and aroma, you need to cut from the centre out. This is easier with a small to medium wheel of soft cheese — you simply cut small triangular wedges. Square or rectangular soft/washed-rind cheeses can also be cut this way as long as they aren't too soft. Long cylindrical cheeses such as provolone can be cut into discs, then into triangles, pyramids into quarters or eighths from the top down, and medium-sized aged cheese into wedges, then again into smaller pieces making sure the range includes the centre out.

There are a few lessons that I've learned over time, but occasionally it's good to break the rules. I have been told that some cheese people don't like when a cheese is shaved, but I love it, especially with most alpine-style cheeses. The texture completely changes and almost becomes a salty, creamy, buttery fudge. Tête de Moine (meaning 'monk's head' in English) is an alpine-style cheese that sits on a special tool called a girolle wheel, which shaves in a circular fashion to resemble the top of a monk's head, hence the name. The nutty, pudgy and pliable rosettes of cheese that are produced from this are so unique. Queen of Corona, a natural-rind goat's cheese that came from Crown Finish Caves via Italy, was another cheese that was also able to have its top curled for dramatic effect and taste. This gives a completely different mouthfeel, aroma and flavour than if you just had a wedge.

Cheese for use in salads and cooking can be shaved, grated, Microplaned, cut, chunked, balled, ribboned and cut in many other ways too. It depends on the application and what you are looking to achieve. I love how cutting cheese in different ways alters the flavour, texture and aromas.

Finely grated Parmigiano-Reggiano and a good nugget of it taste completely different, especially when you get a salty, crunchy tyrosine diamond in the nugget. And while we are here, it should be said that Parmigiano-Reggiano is known as the king of cheese for a reason. It is made with cow's milk, rennet and salt and was created before the invention of refrigeration. It is a beautiful cheese that can be served as it is on a cheese plate at the start or end of the meal. Your new friend, the cheesemonger, will cut it to order for you and you shouldn't buy it grated. You do that fresh.

Eating and enjoying cheese

When chefs put together a menu and serve guests, there is a sequence to the way the food comes out. This is more relevant in sharing, banquet, prix fixe and degustation-style dining, where the food comes out in a progression of dishes, and it's up to the servers to explain the dishes and progression. It is really important to the experience to know how it all pairs and fits within the meal.

Below is a list of how I learned to sequence dishes and food at Cumulus. The lighter, smaller dishes go first, moving to the larger, heavier dishes and proteins to make for a balanced and progressive meal.

Oysters/raw shellfish
Cold snacks
Hot snacks
Cold seafood
Cold meat
Salads/vegetables/cheese
Hot shellfish
Hot fish
Hot chicken/pork
Hot red meat
Smaller before larger
Roast/grilled before braised
Mild before spicy

Eating and enjoying things that make sense and complement each other together, slowly building on your palate, is also a fun way to eat, drink and dine. It's the same with cheese.

Milder cheese to stronger flavours
Younger to older
Lighter styles to the more complex
Goat or sheep before buffalo and cow
Bloomy-rinds before washed-rinds
Washed-rinds before harder
Pasteurised milk before raw milk
Blue cheese last
Soft blues before hard blues

This also helps with pairing beverages and cheese. Lighter, brighter and perhaps bubblier styles of white wines, cider and beer suit the younger bloomy, rich, mouldy styles; bolder beers and sweeter wines suit the funky washed-rinds; moving along the scale into the reds and oxidative wines, which are good with the more aged, firmer, nutty cheeses; and finishing with fortified wines that go well with the blues. Teas, juices, cocktails, whisky and liqueurs can also pair really well with cheese. There are some really unique and beautiful combinations of cheese and beverages out there. Remember, what grows together, goes together and, in the case of washed-rinds, it's best to drink whatever the cheese was washed in, where possible.

Storing cheese

Even after the cheese is matured, cut and served, it is still very much alive and will dry out, deteriorate and go bad if not looked after. Cheese loves, wants and needs moisture – in moderation. After cutting, keep your cheese wrapped in cheese paper, beeswax wraps or aluminium foil if you must. Plastic wrap doesn't allow the cheese to breathe. Storing cheese in a lidded container can build up too much moisture and restart mould growth, as you may notice when you are ageing them, as can keeping too many cheeses together in a container. Keep the lid off if you must, and also keep a rack in the bottom so the cheese isn't sitting in any moisture. Water and cheese don't mix well.

Bring cheese to room temperature before serving.

Cheese that has unwanted mould on it can be trimmed or scraped to use the cheese straight away.

Most household refrigerators have a salad and lettuce crisper drawer in the bottom. These are much better places to keep your cheese than the top shelf, which is usually designated for cheese. The crisper keeps the moisture in better, and is better for storing cheese — wrapped of course.

Fresh cheeses and curds that you make are best kept in sterilised jars and containers in the fridge. By sterilising them you give them the best shelf life possible. As all the dairy you've made doesn't contain stabilisers, thickeners or additives, they may not last as long as store-bought products. They should absolutely taste better and be better for you, though. Keep them clean, use clean utensils and try not to double-dip to help them last longer. Alternatively, eat them fast and make more.

Get creative

I've been a pretty rigid and structured person most of my life — there must be order. With experience and time, I'm learning to ride the wave, which in turn has helped with creativity, understanding, letting go and slowing down.

Sometimes things will go wrong with your cheese, sometimes you will have to call it a loss and move on. Sometimes, however, you may make a discovery and continue down the path of the project and experiment to make something interesting and perhaps unique. Most times though, it will not be as unique as you may think — someone, somewhere has more than likely made a similar mistake and discovery, but we wouldn't have cheese without this process.

At this point I should say again: if in doubt, throw it out. There is a cheese in Sardinia in Italy called casu martzu, which is ripened with maggots. I accidentally made something similar once — that one was a horrible mistake and definitely not for use or experimenting with.

Barring your cheese being harmful to eat, try using the not-so-desirables in recipes that require cooking, such as cheese sauces, and also use the cheese rinds and scraps that you may accumulate. Don't be scared of the rinds; they have so much complexity and flavour and can be used in sauces, soups, custards and other applications. Taste them first, however, as some can be incredibly bitter.

Just think where we would be if those first people never tried milk, transported it, came across rennet, or made and aged cheese. Cook with your cheese, try it in recipes, share it with friends, enjoy the process and have fun with it. The important thing is to learn from the failures and just keep trying.

Write it down

If I had my time over, I'd have books filled with notes, anecdotes, recipes, thoughts, feelings and ideas. Make a chart of your cheesemaking exploits — what works, what doesn't, what you can improve, what you liked and what you didn't. It will help you improve your cheese and cooking. Here are some things you could include in your notes:

- Milk used
- Amount used
- Timings
- Rennet amount
- Temperatures
- Cut size
- Stirring amount and times
- Curd size
- Curd feel
- Hooping time
- Flipping
- Salting
- Washing
- Ageing times

You could also fill notebooks with your cheese-tasting journey, including the names, styles, ages, milks, appearances, aromas, textures and flavour profiles of each cheese. Train your palate and build up your knowledge of cheese.

Find good cheese people

From when I started on this journey to now, I have met and become friends with some very special, beautiful and passionate people. Some I am lucky to call close friends and mentors.

The infectious curiosity I have for cheese is especially evident when I travel to new countries. In late 2015, just as I was embarking on my cheese journey, I visited the United Arab Emirates to see my buddy Stewy Walton, who had invited me over to cook with him on a yacht for the F1 Grand Prix. It was a very busy time for him and his team, but I kept talking to him about cheese and camels.

One day in the midst of the madness, he drove me out in the hot, dusty, desert rain to a dairy and camel farm on the outskirts of Dubai. The drive was absolutely terrifying. It was a surreal experience trying to see through the dusty windscreen of a small food transport van with sporadic drops of rain being smudged across it by the windscreen wipers on high. It was almost like being in a Dalí painting.

When we arrived, Stewy managed to talk us all the way from the carpark onto the factory floor, where we saw people making various kinds of cheese with fresh camel's milk. This was so fascinating because the composition of camel's milk isn't like that of most other milks; rennet doesn't set it and it can be quite a challenge to successfully make a curd from it. I had not heard of camel's milk cheese prior to the trip, let alone seen it being made.

I still laugh when I think about us sitting in the CEO's office, acting like hotshots tasting through their whole range of cheeses while they treated us like royalty. He is a diamond in the desert, that Stewy.

Around the world, and more recently in Australia, cheese people are hosting festivals, parties, competitions and gatherings for other cheese people and anyone who enjoys cheese. It is so exciting to see cheese start to be celebrated here like it is in Europe, the US and around the world.

Going to visit a cheesemaker, farm or farmer's market is one of the best ways to meet people in cheese and dairy. It's also a good opportunity to let them know how much you enjoy their work, with a lot of cheesemakers not getting the opportunity to hear this kind of feedback.

In the US and Europe, there are an amazing number of resources, programs, scholarships and apprenticeships for people to learn more about cheese. In Australia, we are fortunate to have Long Paddock Cheese and The Cheese School Castlemaine in Victoria, which recently opened to help budding cheesemakers learn from industry professionals. For home cheesemakers there are also many resources and classes available, such as the beautiful curd workshops of Kristen Allen, also in Victoria, with many others popping up in various states.

The future of cheese in Australia is an exciting prospect to think about. For more resources about cheese in Australia, New Zealand, the US and UK, see page 216.

Cheesemaking troubleshooting guide

Cheese curd did not set well	Not enough rennet added Check your rennet – too old or weak Chlorine in water – boil and cool Rennet not dispersed properly – stir well Milk freshness issue – use fresh milk Milk too cold or warm – make sure it is the correct setting temperature Temperatures – make your cheese in the mornings (if you make them in the afternoon/evening, the ambient temperature can drop) Cultures are not active – check quality
Curds are breaking up	Poor milk quality Rennet needed more time Calcium deficiency in the milk – fresher milk or add calcium Temperature has fallen – maintain temperature Stirring/handling is too rough
Curds aren't knitting together to hoop	Curds are too cold – maintain the correct temperature
Curds are drooping when hooping	See above The ambient temperature may be too low (make cheese during the day and ensure the room isn't too cold) Acidification too slow
White mould cheese has unwanted mould/damp	Humidity is too high – create a drier environment and/or work cleaner
Slow mould growth	Temperature and humidity too low – increase Cheese is too salty – use less
Washed-rind not orange	Not enough salt – increase Not washing enough – increase
Cheese has small/medium holes/blown up	Coliforms (harmful bacteria) in milk or cross contamination – ensure good milk is being used and clean/sanitise equipment Too much gas/yeast contamination

Glossary

AFFINAGE
The name given to the process and techniques of ageing cheese. The term means 'to refine' and encompasses many unique techniques and skill sets to ripen and age cheese. An art form.

AFFINEUR
An affineur ripens and ages cheese, maturing it from fresh (green) cheese until when it is ready to be eaten using affinage techniques (see also page 22).

BACTERIA
Microscopic single-celled organisms that can produce both positive and negative results depending on the strain in certain conditions. For cheesemaking, lactic bacteria is the most important as it converts lactose into lactic acid.

BASKETS
Small, perforated vessels that are used predominantly for fresher, smaller, softer styles of cheese, such as white mould. They allow for good moisture retention while allowing the whey to drain as the cheese forms an even shape and size.

BLOWING
Excessive gas formed in cheese due to a contamination that causes the cheese to form gas bubbles and blow up.

BREVIBACTERIUM LINENS
A strain of bacteria that gives washed-rind cheese its orange colouring and pungent aromas. Naturally found on human skin, especially the feet.

BRINE
A salt solution used to season and preserve cheese and food. The percentage can range from low to high and is a measurement of salt to water, so 10% brine of 1 litre (34 fl oz/4 cups) would be 100 g (3½ oz) of salt.

BUTTERMILK
The liquid produced once cream is churned into butter.

CALCIUM CHLORIDE
A salt containing calcium — a way of adding calcium to milk for cheesemaking.

CHEESECLOTH
Loosely woven cotton cloth that enables the whey to drain while encasing the curd.

CITRIC ACID
Available powdered or as a liquid to acidify cheese. It also adds acid when used as a seasoning.

CLABBER
A soured thick milk solution that has bacteria present, which can then be used to inoculate, ferment, sour and thicken. This can be used to make cheese and is a naturally occurring process in raw milk.

CLEAN BREAK
The checking of the set curd with a finger, knife or thermometer. A small cut is made to check the set of the curd before cutting (see also page 21).

CREAM
Cream is the fat that sits on top of the milk when settled. It can be taken from the milk (cream), kept in (unhomogenised), mixed through (homogenised) or skimmed from the milk.

- Pouring (single/light) cream is 30–36% fat and has no additives.
- Pure cream is approximately 40% fat with no thickening agents.
- Thick (double/heavy) cream usually has a fat content of approximately 45% or more.
- Clotted cream is thick (double/heavy) cream with a rich flavour that has been slowly caramelised. It is high in fat.
- Thickened (whipping) cream has added gelatine, additives and stabilisers, which make it easier to whip and cook with.

CURD
The solid mass that forms when milk coagulates.

DRAINING/HANGING
The process of removing whey and liquid from curd or mass.

ENZYME
A protein that speeds up a chemical reaction. In cheese, the enzyme rennet speeds up the coagulation process.

GEOTRICHUM CANDIDUM
A strain of white mould bacteria used in white mould, smear-ripened and lactic-set cheese, giving the wrinkles.

GREEN CHEESE
Fresh curds and cheese — when the cheese is just made, before ageing and maturation begin.

HOMOGENISATION
The process of making things uniform. For milk, this is when the cream is dispersed into smaller particles in to the milk to make it all one.

HOOPING
A step of the cheesemaking process where the curds are further separated from the whey into baskets or hoops to allow the curd to form and the whey to continue to run off.

HOOPS
Larger more robust moulds used for larger cheese, allowing the curds to be pressed to push out more whey and moisture, resulting in a firmer cheese.

FOLLOWER
The lid or disc that sits inside the hoop acting as a lid when pressing cheese.

LACTIC ACID
The acid produced during the fermentation process as the bacteria convert sugar (lactose) the milk during cheesemaking.

LACTOSE
The sugar found in milk.

MESOPHILIC BACTERIA
Bacteria that thrive and work in the middle range from 20–32°C (68–90°F), providing acidity and flavour to cheese.

MICROFLORA
A term used to describe the bacteria, yeasts and moulds of milk, cheese or a place that gives cheese its flavour, profile and terroir.

MILK
- RAW milk is just that — nothing added or done to it.
- PASTEURISED milk has been heat-treated to kill off any 'bad' bacteria.
- UNHOMOGENISED milk has the cream on the top.
- HOMOGENISED milk has had any fat and cream evenly distributed through it, so it is uniform.
- SKIM MILK is milk that has had the fat removed in varying degrees.

PASTEURISATION
The heat treatment of milk to destroy pathogens. This can be done at a high temperature for a short time or a lower temperature for a longer time.

PENICILLIUM CANDIDUM
A white mould bacteria found on soft, white mould cheese, helping to soften and ripen the cheese.

PH
The measurement of acid and alkaline with 7 being neutral, lower being acidic and alkaline higher.

RENNET
An enzyme used to set milk, originally found in the stomach of young calves and goat kids. Can also be found in vegetable and microbial form.

RIND
The surface of a cheese that contains mould and bacteria to protect the inside paste.

RIPENING – IN CHEESEMAKING
The term used to describe the period when the milk is coming to temperature and bacterial growth is increasing.

ROOM TEMPERATURE
Cheese is made in warm environments to aid in the bacterial growth and keep them happy. For the home, 20-22°C (68–72°F) is good.

STERILISING
The killing of bacteria and pathogens using boiling hot water.

TOMME
A small semi-hard style cheese, typically made with skim milk on the farm in small batches in the alps of France and Switzerland.

THERMOPHILIC
Bacteria that are active in the higher temperature range – 40–50°C (104–122°F) for curds that are cooked.

WATER BATH
A pot sitting inside a bath, or another pan of water, that allows for indirect heating.

WHEY
The liquid in milk that is left after the casein curd has been coagulated and removed. A clear liquid that contains lactose, protein and water.

Resources

Stephanie Alexander, *The Cook's Companion*, Lantern, 2004
David Asher, *The Art of Natural Cheesemaking*, Chelsea Green Publishing, 2015
Ricki Carroll, *Home Cheese Making*, Storey, 2002
Catherine Donnelly, *The Oxford Companion to Cheese*, Oxford University Press, 2016
Anthony Femia, *Maker & Monger, Talk Dairy to Me*, SomeKind Press, 2020
Justin Gellatly, *Bread, Cake, Doughnut, Pudding*, Penguin, 2016
Nick Haddow, *Milk Made*, Hardie Grant Books, 2016
Bronwen & Francis Percival, *Reinventing the Wheel*, Bloomsbury/Sigma, 2017
Anne Saxelby, *The New Rules of Cheese*, Clarkson Potter/Ten Speed, 2021

FRIENDS, PLACES, PEOPLE AND SOURCES OF INSPIRATION

New York, USA
Murray's Cheese Shop
Saxelby's
Chef's Collective & Chris Killoran
Crown Finish Caves – Benton Brown and Susan Boyle (now closed)
Bedford Cheese Shop
C. Heese Cheese – Caroline Heese

Indiana, USA
Capriole Goat Cheese

Vermont, USA
Jasper Hill Farm

USA and beyond
Milk Trekker aka Trevor Warmedahl

Canada
The Black Sheep School of Cheesemaking – David Asher

London & UK
Neals Yard Dairy
St James Cheese - Martin Gott
St Jude Cheese - Blake Bowden

Madrid, Spain
Formaje — Clara Díez

L'Etivav, Switzerland
Pascal Guenat

Paris, France
Taka & Vermo

Melbourne, Australia
Maker & Monger — Anthony Femia

Castlemaine, Victoria
Long Paddock and The Cheese School

Sutton Grange, Victoria
Holy Goat Cheese

Bellarine, Australia
Drysdale Cheeses

Yarra Valley, Victoria
Stone and Crow — Jack Holman

Nannup, West Australia
Cambray Cheese — Tom & Maddie Wilde

Sydney, Australia
Wildflower Brewing and Blending - Topher Boehm
Willowbrae cheese - Daniel Thaine

Kiama, New South Wales
The Pines — Kel and Mahlah Grey

UAE
Camelicious
Cheese and pickle centre, Dubai
Stuart Walton

ONLINE EQUIPMENT AND TOOLS

Cheese links — Australia
www.cheeselinks.com.au

Cheesemaking.com — US & Canada
www.cheesemaking.com

Glengarry Cheesemaking
www.glengarrycheesemaking.on.ca

Cheesemaking shop — UK
www.cheesemaking.co.uk

About the author

Colin Wood started his culinary path in Perth before rising to the ranks of Head Chef at Cumulus Inc. in Melbourne's CBD and then Development Chef for Andrew McConnell. It was during this time that Wood uncovered his passion for cheesemaking, and, under the tutelage of cheesemaker Richard Thomas, Wood refined his craft and established the first in-house Dairy Program for Cutler & Co.

In 2017, Wood headed to New York City where he was the Culinary Director for Ignacio Mattos at Flora Bar, Estela and Altro Paradiso, before returning to Australia and establishing cheesemaking collaborations with Poly, AP Bakery and Wildflower Brewing & Blending in Sydney.

Acknowledgements

This book would not have been possible without the support, encouragement, persistence, friendship and guidance of many.

To Rushani Epa and the team at Hardie Grant, thank you for taking a chance on a broken man in the back alley of Melbourne CBD. I have gained so much out of this experience, most of all, a kind and caring friend.

Ariane Klepac, the voice of reason. Thank you for putting the puzzle, words and, at times, me, nicely together.

Rob Palmer and Lucy Tweed, a real-life dream team. Thank you for your input, your style, your counsel and for bringing the cheese and food to life on these beautiful pages.

To Mum, you have been, and always will be, a source of inspiration, encouragement, wisdom and light. Nothing is too hard, too big, too scary or too much for you.

To my dad, John. Thank you for all those early-morning lifts, the wake-up calls, the teachings, the listening and instilling a sense of discipline, persistence and drive in me. I am who I am because of this and you.

My siblings, Alison, Suzi and Mick, thank you for the never-ending support and for being my biggest champions since forever. Thank you also to the next chapter of fans – one day I hope they'll appreciate my 'stinky cheese' too.

To Ramesh and Suzie, thank you for being there for us always. And a special thanks too for the beautiful title. It made sense when you said it at lunch, and even more so now. There really is always room for cheese.

To all the chefs and restaurant people who have given me a shot, who have inspired, trained, schooled, influenced and mentored me over the years. I've learnt a lot. Thank you.

Ignacio and the teams at Estela, Altro and the shuttered Flora Bar – those times were some of the most challenging yet rewarding. The intensity, focus and drive is exemplary. It's left a mark on me. I'll use it to keep making cheese and make it well. Thank you for taking a chance on me and your continued support.

Sammy Lawrence, thank you for being one of the best cheerleaders and friends anyone could ask for. Your humility, honesty, passion, talent and enthusiasm is unrivalled.

To Topher, if everyone had someone like you in their corner, the world would be a brighter place. I had hoped to include a recipe for you in these pages, but I guess that will have to be for book two. Maybe with one of our own cheeses.

Thanks to the friends and family that have been a big part of the journey, some from the start – Caleb Baker, Stewy Walton, Casey McDonald, Anthony Femia, Liz Carey and Paul Guiney, Caroline Heese, Daniel Eddy, Mat Lindsay and Dougal Muffet.

To Ben Evans, this book and story may have taken a different path if it weren't for you and St David's Dairy. Thank you for encouraging me to live the cream.

To Richard Thomas, this book would not have been written without you. I hope I have made you proud. When you inoculated me with that cheese bug all those years ago, you got it so perfectly right. The conditions, timing and knowledge of the cheesemaker were all set up to make the good bugs flourish. And man, they did.

And to my wife, Andrea, thank you for sharing your dream with me, for encouraging and helping me to be better, for your patience, for your kindness and support. I love you.

Index

Rind and jelly.

Published in 2023 by Hardie Grant Books, an imprint of Hardie Grant Publishing

Hardie Grant Books (Melbourne)
Wurundjeri Country
Building 1, 658 Church Street
Richmond, Victoria 3121

Hardie Grant Books (London)
5th & 6th Floors
52–54 Southwark Street
London SE1 1UN

hardiegrant.com/books

Hardie Grant acknowledges the Traditional Owners of the Country on which we work, the Wurundjeri People of the Kulin Nation and the Gadigal People of the Eora Nation, and recognises their continuing connection to the land, waters and culture. We pay our respects to their Elders past and present.

NATIONAL LIBRARY OF AUSTRALIA
A catalogue record for this book is available from the National Library of Australia

There's Always Room for Cheese
ISBN 978 1 74379 876 8

10 9 8 7 6 5 4 3 2 1

Commissioning Editor: Rushani Epa
Editor: Ariana Klepac
Design Manager: Kristin Thomas
Designer: Claire Orrell
Photographer: Rob Palmer
Stylist: Lucy Tweed
Production Manager: Todd Rechner
Production Coordinator: Jessica Harvie

Colour reproduction by Splitting Image Colour Studio
Printed in China by Leo Paper Products LTD.

FSC www.fsc.org MIX Paper | Supporting responsible forestry FSC® C020056

The paper this book is printed on is from FSC® -certified forests and other sources. FSC® promotes environmentally responsible, socially beneficial and economically viable management of the world's forests.